Job Hawk

A Job Searching Blueprint For Any Economic Environment
By Matthew J. Kelly

319 Publishing Company
Copyright © 2016 by Matthew J. Kelly

This book is dedicated to my wife Hilary Kelly, who has given me the utmost support through the highs and lows of my professional career. Her decision to leave her own job so I could advance my career was an incredibly selfless act. I'll never forget that.

Preface: Getting to know your author

Since you're now about to vest some of your valuable time in reading this book, it's only appropriate that I take this opportunity to introduce myself, and explain what qualifies me to educate you in the art of job searching. I'll be candid, I've never taken any instructional courses in job searching nor have I read any books on the subject, but I will say my record speaks for itself. Between 2009 (described as the "toughest labor market in at least 25 years" by the Wall St. Journal[1]), when the Great Financial Recession engulfed the global economy, and 2013 when the domestic job market was still feeling the hangover from the recession, I successfully completed three job searches. With each job search I was able to land a highly sought after role, and more importantly, I was advancing in my career. Given that I conducted three job searches in that five year stretch, and a total of six job searches over the course of my twelve year career, you may be drawn to the conclusion that I actually enjoy job searching. Nothing could be further from the truth. I can think of an infinite number of activities I'd rather be doing with my time. However, as fate would have it I was continuously finding myself in the midst of a job search. If I wanted to elevate my career to the next level I had no choice but to excel in job searching. And excel I did, but not without overcoming a steep learning curve. My goal in writing Job Hawk is to help you accelerate through that learning curve and secure a great job so you can get back to all the other activities you love in life.

Now everyone has their own story as to how their job search commenced. Perhaps you were laid off, maybe you were just bored with the job you've been in for ten years, maybe you saw your position as a dead-end, or maybe you were a stay-at-home mom returning to the work force after your children started grade school. We all have our own reasons, and to be honest it doesn't really matter how you got to this position, you're here now.

My story dates back to 2009. In January of that year, at the peak of the Great Financial Recession, I was laid off. I was one of the lucky 791,000[2] individuals in the United States that were laid off that month, the second worst month of job losses during the recession. I was working for a commercial real estate investment firm in downtown Boston at the time, and when the market went south, so too did my job. I was out of work for about

---

[1] Murray, S. "The Curse of the Class of 2009." *Wall St. Journal* 9 May 2009

[2] Bureau of Labor Statistics. "Change in Total Non-farm Payroll Employment" <http://data.bls.gov/timeseries/CES0000000001?output_view=net_1mth>

three months before landing a position with a publicly traded energy firm just west of Boston. Let me repeat that because you may have missed it, it took me just three months to find a highly sought after job in the worst recession since the Great Depression. To give you a sense of how competitive the job market was back then, a colleague of mine at the time, who worked in the human resources division our company, told me the position I had just landed had drawn hundreds of applications. This was not entirely surprising to me given the velocity of layoffs that had been taking place in Massachusetts and the country as a whole.

After about a year it became clear to me that there was not a long term career path for me with this particular company, and I knew it was time for me to move on. I commenced job searching in April of 2010, and landed a new position by August of that year. So once again, with the economy still reeling from the recession, and unemployment standing at 9.9%[3], it took me only four months to land a new job. Mind you, during that four month job search I was also working full time and studying for a professional designation, so given the circumstances, four months was exceptionally fast.

The new position I secured was with the U.S. Department of Energy ("DOE") in Washington, DC. I was a bit more cautious in my search in 2010, and was keenly focused on finding a position, and a company, that ensured career growth. My error in judgment relating to my 2009 job search was that I was more focused on the job itself, and neglected to take into account whether there was actually a long term career for me at the company. For the first year and a half my role with the DOE was completely satisfying, in fact it was better than I could have imagined. I was in the world of energy banking, the work content was interesting, the job was dynamic, and I was surrounded by talented colleagues. I distinctly recall walking down C Street one morning on the way to my office and thinking to myself, "this is the type of work I could see myself doing for the rest of my career." The salary at the DOE was only marginally better than what I was making at the energy company in Massachusetts, but I was so engrossed in my work that the long hours and mediocre salary were but a secondary thought. For the first time in my career I realized I didn't need to make a large sum of money to love my job. This was an essential career lesson I learned. I had never been in a job that I loved so much, and salary became but a second thought, not the primary motivator to show up each morning.

---

[3] Bureau of Labor Statistics. "Unemployment Rate" <http://data.bls.gov/timeseries/LNS14000000>

Unfortunately, the satisfaction I had once been receiving through my position at the DOE slowly started to diminish. Turmoil in Congress relating to budgetary issues, and some inaccurate and politically influenced bad press, put the future prospects of my division in jeopardy. One day I showed up at work and everything seemed to change. It was if the division was trying to move forward, but with the parking brake on. The bureaucracy and red tape of government became too difficult to muddle through. About two years into the job, the work flow started to slow down, and the division became bloated. With little direction from DOE leadership on the future of my division, I realized it was an appropriate time to take the next step in my career, which unfortunately for me meant another job search.

In July of 2012, I began job searching for the third time in just over three years. I was not happy about it. I knew this would be the most challenging job search of my career thus far. I was determined, and committed, to landing a position where I could spend the next 10 years of my career. Once this job search was completed I did not even want to think about job searching again for the foreseeable future. The only way to ensure that would happen was to secure my ideal job with a company that laid the framework for a rewarding career. So after a vacation to California during the week of July 4th 2012, I came back to DC, and began my job search, and that search did not end until April of 2013. I was offered a position back in Boston with a well known, well respected, financial institution. I am quite certain this is the only position I have ever been offered in which the job, salary, and career potential all met my expectations.

That folks, is my story. I'm not a career coach, I'm not a recruiter, and I don't work in human resources or at a staffing agency. I'm simply a guy who's done a lot of interviewing over the last twelve years, and I've gotten pretty good at the game. This book will share the very same methods and techniques I used to conduct three successful job searches during the worst of economic conditions.

Before we get started, I think it's important to discuss a few foundational rules. I have no doubt in the efficacy of my techniques, but you, as a job seeker, must also be realistic in your expectations. By that I mean if your highest level of education is a high school diploma, it's unlikely you will be hired as the CFO of a publicly traded Fortune 500 company. I know that's an extreme example, but you get the point. So make sure that the positions you are seeking are in line with your education, work experience, and are conducive to your overall lifestyle (e.g., don't look at investment banking jobs if you only want to work 40 hours a week). This doesn't mean you need to be a perfect match for a given job, but you will need to be able to demonstrate how your background and strengths will help you excel in the position you're pursuing. We will work on this together.

The next rule I want to reinforce is that there is no substitute for hard work and perseverance when it comes to a job search. I say this because at some point during your search you may feel frustration, despair, and that your quest for a new job is a hopeless cause. These are all normal feelings, and you are certainly not alone in having such feelings. God knows that I've doubted my own ability to secure a new job at times. However, I stick to the game plan, persevere, and at the end of the day, it's always worked out for me. I say this to you because hard work and commitment is a requirement for a successful job search, not an option.

The final concept I want to convey is best told through a brief story. I completed my graduate studies at the Carroll Graduate School of Management at Boston College in April 2009. At my graduation, the commencement speaker stated one line that has somehow become engrained in my ongoing pursuit of career development. The line was, and I'm paraphrasing, "sometimes to get ahead in life, you will need to place yourself in uncomfortable positions." I don't remember that commencement speaker's name, nor do I remember anything else he said that rainy day. Yet that one line stuck with me and today I consider it gospel. So be prepared that during your job search, you may at times be placed in situations that are uncomfortable relative to your day to day routine. I believe it is the fear of venturing into the unknown that keeps millions of people in their current jobs, even when they feel unfulfilled in their careers. Are you willing to step out of your comfort zone?

Before we begin I would like to leave you with a quote from a favorite artist of mine, Kid Rock - "You get what you put in, and people get what they deserve."

Introduction

I have written this book for those of you out there that are motivated, ready to begin a job search, but don't know where to start, and are feeling a bit overwhelmed. If you fall into this category then take a deep breath, you're not alone. You've also picked a fine book to read which is going to provide you with a blueprint for securing your next job. Why is this book different than every other "job searching" book on the market? Simple, your author is someone who has actually gone to battle in the job market, three times between 2009 and 2013, and won every single time. If you were to look at job searching tutorial books that are on the market today, you will find that most are authored by individuals that have careers in human resources, motivational speaking, career blogging, or guidance counseling. Ask yourself this though, have any of those authors successfully completed a job search starting from ground zero in the midst of a recession, or are they simply waxing poetic about what they perceive would make for a successful search? This book will provide you with a step by step guide on how to tackle your upcoming job search utilizing the very same techniques I have used throughout my adventures in job searching.

Before you invest any more time in this book I have a prerequisite, which I mentioned in the preface, but it's worth repeating: You must be motivated because job searching is NOT easy. In fact job searching can be mentally and physically exhausting, it's a grind. However, a successful job search can lead to a very rewarding outcome. So don't fool yourself, if you're not motivated to search, or if you're not fully committed at this point in time, then come back another day. Everyone has their reasons why now is not the right time. However, if you are motivated, and committed, then what are we waiting for? Let's get to it and get a job.

Part 1: Pre-interview

Chapter 1: General guidelines

Job searching is now your new favorite hobby. In other words, job searching is going to consume most all of your extra time. If you are unemployed, then job searching should consume most all of your time, as if it were a full time job in itself. Yes, you heard me correctly. If you're unemployed you should be job searching 9am-5pm Monday through Friday. I realize you may have children, an elderly parent, tickets to a concert, or a road race to run. Unfortunately, as much of an inconvenience as it may be to your current situation, your job search needs to take top priority, and others around you must be aware of this, and should be supportive of you. If you choose not to place your job search as the top priority in your life, the duration of time it will take you to find a job, in all likelihood, will be drastically extended.

Let me tell you a quick story to illustrate the point. A very close friend of mine (we'll call him Gavin) graduated from a top-25 full-time MBA program in May of 2012. Gavin had great work experience, and a solid educational background. Given that I've known him since eighth grade, I can also say with confidence that he's a diligent worker and motivated. Three months prior to graduating from his MBA program, Gavin commenced job searching. Those three months of job searching led to dead ends, so upon graduating in May of 2012, Gavin made job searching his new full time job. His days and nights were consumed with job searching, and I observed it all from the sidelines. Let's fast forward this story - Gavin did not land a full time position until March of 2013. The bottom line is it took Gavin, a highly marketable job candidate, a full year to secure employment when he placed job searching as the number one priority in his life, and had not a single distraction. Imagine if Gavin was engaged in job searching activities for only an hour or two a day, his search would have undoubtedly dragged on longer.

As another example, the last time I commenced a full blown job search it too became the top priority in my life, even above my position at the time. There was rarely a day that went by that I did not perform some activity related to the search, and it still lasted 10 months.

You must get in the habit of conducting some job searching activity every single day, no matter how small. Eventually it will become second nature and seem less of a chore, and more of a way of life. Assuming you are currently employed in a full-time job, I recommend 1.5-2 hours of job searching activity every weekday, and 3 hours of job searching activity each weekend day (that totals 13-16 hours per week).   If you are out of work, your entire day (7-8 hours per day) should be filled with job searching activities. Some of you may be wondering if it is actually possible to fill up 8 hours a day with job searching activities. My answer is an unequivocal, "Yes." When I was out of work after getting laid-off in 2009, I filled every day (8 hours/day, Monday through Friday, for 3 months) with job searching activities, just like my friend Gavin. Sacrifices will be required, and that is why it's so important to have the support of those close to you (e.g., girlfriend, wife, parents, friends, etc.) prior to diving into the job search. Now I'm sure many of you reading this book have a friend or family member that was able to find a new job quickly once they embarked on a job search. Sure, you too may be lucky enough to find employment after a few weeks of searching, and I hope that is the case, but if you look at the statistics you'll realize you're likely in for a much longer journey. In fact, according to the Bureau of Labor Statistics, as of December 2014 the average length of unemployment in the United States was 33 weeks[4] (that's over 8 months).

It's also important you establish daily goals for yourself during your job search. Here are some examples of goals you may try to achieve:

1. Send out (x) resumes per day
2. Apply to (x) jobs per day
3. Have (x) networking calls per day
4. Identify (x) companies per day that may offer a position that you're interested in pursuing
5. Prepare for an interview (note that this task can and should be done irrespective of whether of not you have an interview lined up).

    X = # of your choice

I have found that establishing daily goals in prior searches kept me focused, and more importantly, gave me a sense of accomplishment. Without establishing daily goals, it becomes very easy for days and weeks of job searching to seemingly pass by, leaving you with the feeling that you've made little to no progress. My recommendation is at the end of each day take 5-10 minutes to establish your goals for the following day. In doing so you will start each day with a fresh game plan. If you complete the daily goals you've established for yourself you will be making progress in your search, whether you realize it or not. In the following chapter we will work

---

[4] Bureau of Labor Statistics. "Unemployed Persons by Duration of Unemployment" <http://www.bls.gov/news.release/empsit.t12.htm>

on establishing your job log, which will assist in keeping track of your daily goals.

Chapter 2: Prerequisites to job searching

Placing yourself on the right path for a successful job search requires preparation, and that preparation is likely to be time consuming. In fact, I spent nearly a month preparing before launching my last job search. You may think that sounds a bit excessive, but think of it like this. You wouldn't jump into a long distance race before doing some level of preparation first, right? Of course not. You'd buy the right running clothes, acquire the appropriate sneakers, find a training route, perhaps lose some weight, make a running playlist, and you'd stretch….and that's all before even starting to train for the race. It's the same concept with a job search, you can't just jump right in, or it could get ugly pretty fast.

Your very first task of job searching prep work is defining the job you are seeking. Consider each of the following when undertaking this task (this list is not all inclusive or in any particular order of priority):

1. industry
2. salary
3. title
4. division of a company
5. preference of management style
6. location of a company
7. size of a company
8. commuting distance
9. position you want five years down the road, and which job(s) will get you there
10. what you don't want in a job
11. job function and responsibilities[5]
12. willingness to pursue a transitory job
13. what positions align with your personal interests as well as your education/training

The list of job characteristics I put forth is not all inclusive, but rather a baseline. I encourage you to develop your own list with as many job characteristics as necessary so that it will help you classify the type of job you are seeking. The more specific you can be in terms of what you are

---

[5] There is a distinct difference between "job function" and "job responsibilities". A job function is more general in nature where as job responsibilities are more specific in nature. As an example, financial planning and analysis is a job function. Presenting to the board of directors on the upcoming fiscal budget is a job responsibility.

looking for in a job, the better off you will be.   Also, be honest with yourself, and be thoughtful when answering these questions.   One flaw I identified in my last job search is that I would occasionally apply for a job that matched my qualifications, but I had little interest in the job itself.   I attribute this flaw to not clearly defining what I was seeking in a job. Trust me, the last place you want to find yourself is interviewing for a position that is of no interest to you.

If you find that the characteristics you've outlined are yielding a wide range of job possibilities, in various industries, ask yourself this, "Will each of these potential jobs inevitably lead me to a long and rewarding career?" Perhaps the reason your answers have yielded a wide range of positions or industries is because you're feeling desperate for a job, and not because of a sincere interest in a particular position. As a recruiter once told me, "you want to marry a job, not have a one night stand."   The pre-screening questions will help you avoid pursuing jobs that aren't aligned with your long term interests in addition to saving you time and preventing you from wasting effort and brain power.

The most time consuming exercise prior to commencing your job search is building your resume. This book is not intended to provide you with the techniques of building a resume, as that topic has been widely covered by people that are far better resume writers than myself. One can do a google search and bring up countless resume templates that are perfectly adequate. The point I do want to get across to you is that you must have a resume fully prepared before you jump into networking or scouring the internet for jobs. Scrambling to pull together a resume is not in your best interest.   It will likely lead to a poorly constructed document that does not appropriately reflect your job history.   Remember, you only have one chance to make a first impression, and often times in job searching, it's your resume that is making the initial impression.

I have just two rules regarding the construction of your resume. The first is to keep it short and direct. I don't care if you've had five jobs or more, your resume should be no more than one page.   Why?   The answer is simple, humans have short attention spans.   Furthermore, keeping your resume to one page will force you as the author to get your point across in as few as words as possible, and managers love efficiency.   I can sense your frustration here, and trust me I've been in your shoes.   For someone who loves to write, getting my resume down to one page was a difficult hurdle to overcome.   My second rule is never lie on your resume.   Construct your resume under the assumption that at some point during the interview process a reference of yours will need to verify the content within you resume.   By lying, you are indirectly also asking your reference to lie. This could place you in a very precarious position.

Finally, as much as you may think you're a good writer, have a colleague or friend read your resume to identify any spelling and grammatical errors. Even if the document contains no errors, simply ask a friend for recommendations because a concept that may appear clear to you may appear convoluted to another reader.

Chapter 3: The world of networking

I'll let the cat out of the bag, you are going to find your next job through social networking[6]. Now before we go any further down this rabbit hole let's define "social networking." According to Merriam-Webster, social networking is the creation and maintenance of business relationships. You may hear that word "networking" and cringe but don't worry, you're probably not alone. Networking, if you've never done it, can be intimidating. The good news is once you start networking, it gets much easier, almost to the point where it becomes second nature. The best jobs come through networking, and the more you network, the quicker your job search will come to an end. I graduated college in 2002 and have landed six jobs over the past 14 years (yikes, I can't believe I've been out of college 14 years). Do you know how many of those six jobs were sourced via networking? The answer: every single one. Is this coincidence? I don't think so. During each of those six job searches I attempted to source positions through a number of different avenues, yet every time networking proved to be my yellow brick road. This has led me to the conclusion that networking yields the highest probability of landing a great position in the least amount of time. Look, if you simply flat out refuse to network, you may as well cut your losses and put this book down right now. However if you're willing to give networking a shot I'll show you how it's done, effectively, and naturally.

The first step in networking is finding the right people to network with. Colleagues, friends, or advisors may encourage you to attend a career fair or perhaps a social networking event (e.g., a regional alumni reunion), to enhance your network. I would advise the exact opposite. General networking events, and career fairs, are not an efficient use of your time, and are incredibly awkward, even for a great networker like myself. I can say this with conviction because I used to attend these events. My advice to you is not to attend a single "networking event". When I say "networking event", I'm referring to gatherings where large numbers of random people from a wide variety of industries gather together in hopes that discussions amongst one another lead to employment. Networking events include industry social events, alumni networking events, and of course, the most dreadful of all, the general job career fair. I think career fairs are fine if you're a college or graduate student, but if you're already out in the work force, do not waste your time attending these events. Now that I've gone on

---

[6] I will use "social networking" and "networking" interchangeably

my rant about networking events I owe you an explanation as to why I am so opinionated on this topic.

I speak from the experience of having attended a number of these networking events over the years. There are two primary reasons why I think networking events/career fairs are a poor use of your time. First, you don't know who is going to be attending these events. Let's say, for an example, you go to an alumni networking event sponsored by your college. Let's also assume you are currently engaged in a job search seeking a position in corporate development within the energy sector. Now what are the odds that someone attending that event is going to be able to assist you in securing that corporate development position within the energy sector? I'd be willing to bet that there is a 10% chance that someone at that event would be able to assist you in that specific search. Furthermore, even in the low probability scenario that there was someone at that event that could assist you in securing that job in energy corporate development, what are the odds that you will actually bump into that person at the event, and start speaking with them? I'd say your odds of speaking to that individual is also roughly 10%. Therefore, the conditional probability of someone attending the event that can assist you in your job search **and** actually speaking to that individual, is around 1%. You have to remember that networking events typically last 1.5-2 hours. During that time period you may end up engaged in a meaningful dialogue with five people. The point is, that simply based on the duration of the event, you will be unable able to speak with the large majority of people in attendance. There is no reason why you should be spending hours upon hours of your time attending these events with such unappealing odds in your corner. There are far more important activities which you should be engaged in.

The second reason why attending networking events is a fruitless mission is because trying to engage someone in a conversation can feel forced and may prove to be a challenge. My experience at networking events is that the person you really would like to speak with is surrounded by numerous other people, just like you, who are vying for that highly coveted individual's time. Envision a scene where five or more people have formed a circle around a single individual, with each groveling to get the man-in-the-middle's attention. I've seen this situation unfold before my own eyes. In fact, I've even been one of those individuals in the circle battling for face time. It's so unnatural and awkward. I don't want to see you go down that road. To effectively network with someone you need to be able to connect with them on a personal level, you need their undivided time and attention, and you need to be able to ask them thought provoking questions. You will be far more efficient in accomplishing this task through a one-on-one conversation. Plain and simple, you need to create your own networking event, where the only two people in attendance are you and the person you want to speak with.

You may be thinking to yourself, "I'm so desperate for a job that I'm willing to consider just about any industry or line of work. Maybe career fairs are worth my while." While your intent is genuine, I whole heartedly advise against conducting an unfocused job search. Jumping into an unfocused job search where every conceivable job is on the table is bound to end ugly. Moreover, if you are truly lost in your search and uncertain about what job you should be pursuing, there are other methods that can be implemented to get you on the right path. We'll discuss these shortly. The bottom line is stay focused and specific in your search and don't get lured into networking events. If you are still skeptical of my argument, which some of you may be, then I suggest attending one networking event or career fair for yourself, and you will see that my comments are justified.

Tactical Networking

First and foremost, the key to successful networking is finding the right people to network with, and I'm going to help you identify those individuals. During my last job search I used three tools to assist me in identifying people within my network that could assist me in my job search. I will go through each of them at length, so settle in. The first, and by far the most utilized, was Linkedin (www.linkedin.com). Linkedin is an excellent networking tool, and I have been using the service since 2009 (the service was launched in 2003). For those of you who may not be familiar with Linkedin, it's a social network site, similar to Facebook, but on a professional level. Members on Linkedin post about trends in their industry, rather than alerting their network about the bachelor party they attended in Las Vegas or the unforgettable restaurant they dined in the previous evening.

The benefit of Linkedin, from a networking perspective is that nearly all users create a detailed searchable profile which describes their job history and education. I like to think of Linkedin as a vast database of searchable resumes. For instance, let's revert to that hypothetical example of someone looking for a corporate development position within the energy industry. Furthermore, let's say that this individual is only interested in positions in San Francisco. This would be a very straight forward search on Linkedin. Once you entered your criteria into Linkedin's search engine, the algorithm would return all individuals in San Francisco that are currently engaged in, or were previously employed in, corporate development within the energy industry. Think about how much more effective and how much time you will save using Linkedin rather than trying to find that elusive person at a networking event. We're comparing typewriters to word processing applications, horse and carriages to gas powered vehicles, hot air balloon to Gulfstream jets. Okay, I think you get the point. Networking events, in my opinion, are going the way of VCRs and cassette players.

You must sign up and utilize Linkedin as part of your job search, it's not even a question. Linkedin's basic service is free, however my requirement is that you sign up for Linkedin's premium service, or more specifically the "Career" package which is currently $29.99/month[7]. First let me be clear, I have absolutely no personal or professional affiliation with Linkedin or anyone that works at Linkedin. I am simply someone who has used the service since 2009, and view the service as a necessity for an effective job search. Back in 2009, when I first started using Linkedin, many of today's premium features were free, but due to popularity, those features come at a cost. Before you totally disregard the concept of paying for Linkedin's premium service let me make my case. Linkedin's free service will allow you to identify the people that you need to be networking with, which is half the battle. What the free service doesn't provide is those individuals' contact information. Of course you may already know some of these individuals on Linkedin that you want to speak with, and have your own means of acquiring their contact information, but what if you don't? By paying the $29.99/per month subscription fee, the premium service enables you to "Inmail" (Linkedin's version of email) up to 3 people per month through the Linkedin portal. If for some reason you were unable to utilize your 3 Inmails in a given month (the chances of this are slim) they would accrue up to a period of 90 days. In other words, you have up to 90 days to use Inmails before they expire. There are a couple of nuances to be aware of when using the premium service. If you reach out to someone via Inmail and they don't respond, then you lose that Inmail. However, if you reach out to someone via Inmail and they do respond, then that Inmail is credited back to your account and can be used again. This forces job seekers to send high quality Inmails to Linkedin members. You may be having concerns that there won't be any people, or enough people, on Linkedin that would be helpful to you in your job search, and justify the monthly payment. Linkedin has over 400 million users at the time of this writing, and I can't think of a single one of my friends or colleagues who is not a member. The odds are in your favor that Linkedin will have members that you need to be speaking with.

I realize spending $30/month is an added expense which can be difficult, particularly if you're out of a job. However, put the fee into perspective. Think about how much you spend on discretionary items each month

---

[7] Quote as of December 11, 2016

between eating out, the movies, guitar lessons, the gym, purchasing music, beer, shoes, or that subscription to Netflix. In the overall scheme of things $30/month is a small amount to pay for a service that can have such a significant impact on the direction of your career. The return on investment is through the roof, in my opinion. Moreover, Linkedin's premium account fees are a tax deductible item, so depending which tax bracket you're in, you could be paying as little as $18/month.

The second tool you need to be using to develop your network is your alma mater's alumni database. These days all colleges and graduate schools (some High Schools too) have searchable databases which contain basic alumni contact information (e.g., date of graduation, major, most recent place of employment, and contact information). The best part about utilizing these services are that they're free (well maybe not entirely free, after all you did pay tens of thousands of dollars for that hard earned degree). In fact, before Linkedin was even launched, I networked into my first job using my college's alumni database. Alumni databases have certainly improved since those days. When I attended college (class of '02), alumni information was stored in stacks of 3-ring binders in the career service center. That seems archaic now, but that's how it worked, and not all that long ago. I literally fingered through hundreds of pages of alumni profiles looking for people to contact. Of course today, alumni databases are all on-line and search friendly.

A technique I frequently used during my last job search involved identifying an alumnus through Linkedin (yes, you can search the Linkedin database by school name too), and then acquire that individuals contact information via my alumni database. The benefit of using this technique is two-fold. First, you will find that Linkedin's searching capabilities are far more powerful than the searching capabilities of a school's alumni database. Second, by sourcing contact information through an alumni database you won't have to use an "Inmail" (which has an implicit cost to it). The point is if you are able to secure an individual's contact information outside of Linkedin then by all means do so, and save those Inmails for when you really need them. I will point out though that the response rate for me was always stronger when reaching out to an alumni through Linkedin as opposed to sourcing and contacting someone through my alumni database. The reason is quite logical. Most individuals on Linkedin are using the service for purposes of networking, so when someone reaches out to them, particularly an alumnus, they are typically receptive to an inquiry. On the other hand, schools will often have all alumni contact info available to current and former students unless an alumnus proactively reaches out to the school's career center and tells the department to remove their contact information from public viewing. The point here is that there is the possibility that individuals you contact via your school's alumni database don't want to network with you (don't take it personally), in fact they may not want to network with any alumni at all.

Therefore try my strategy, it works. Find an alum you would like to speak with via Linkedin (remember they're on Linkedin because they DO want to network, just like you) and then procure their email address through the school's alumni database. This was a very effective technique for me which I would use for contacting alumni from both my undergraduate and graduate schools. Another way to preserve your Inmails is to keep an eye out for Linkedin users that provide their email address within the body of their profile. This is common, so take advantage of emailing when you have the opportunity, and save those Inmails for when you need them.

And finally, in addition to Linkedin and your alma mater's alumni database, you should be using industry trade groups to originate networking leads. During my last job search I was living in Washington, DC however I was looking to relocate to Boston, Massachusetts. I was also seeking positions specifically in financial services. Therefore I joined a Boston based finance trade group called the Boston Security Analysts Society ("BSAS"). By joining the BSAS I had access to the contact information of all active members of the organization as well as select job postings. You will need to do some leg work on your own to find out which trade groups are out there and best suited for your needs, but make no mistake, they're out there.

Make sure you are thoughtful about the organization(s) you join so you get the most bang for your buck. Before joining a trade group ask yourself a few questions - Is the organization I'm joining catered specifically to the same geographic area as my job search? Does the organization have a database with members' contact information readily available? Is the organization I'm about to join well respected within my target industry? Does the organization have a deep member base? The answer to all these questions should be "yes". Typically these organizations, especially the good ones, will charge an annual fee to become a member. The trade group I joined was $150/year (or less than $13/month). I know, another expense!

Let's try to put these expenditures into perspective. Say someone approached you today and made you an offer. The offer is you could have the precise job you are actively seeking, but only for a fee. How much would you be willing to pay? I'll be honest, for me, the number would have four zeros behind it. That's the truth. Now when I compare that to the $30/month for Linkedin, or $150/year to join a professional organization, the cumulative amount spent, when put into perspective, is relatively small.

So what can you expect to get out of joining a professional trade group? First, once you are an official member of the organization, you can add the organization to your resume, which shows employers you are dialed in to the industry. Second, the organization will give you access to its member database which should be searchable by name, position, or company. This will be a source of fresh networking leads. Finally, the organization you join will likely host events (e.g., networking events, industry speakers, field trips, etc.) and by becoming a member of the organization you will likely receive a discounted fare to attend such events. To cut to the chase though, the contact information of fellow members is really what you're paying for here. Moreover, if the organization that you're thinking about joining doesn't provide you with a member database, then I would recommend passing, and try to find another that does.

So there you have it folks, the three primary sources I used to originate networking opportunities: 1. Linkedin 2. College and graduate school alumni databases 3. Professional trade groups. Between those three sources you will have enough networking opportunities to keep you busy for a long time.

The Company List

Now that you have classified the industry, position, and type of company you would like to pursue, you must identify your target universe of companies. This involves listing every single company, within your target geographic area, which could potentially offer the job you want. This process doesn't need to be complex. It simply entails writing out company names. There is no right number that you should be looking to achieve, it all depends on the position and industry you are pursuing within your geographic target. If you're pursuing investment banking jobs in Mt. Shasta, CA, then you likely won't come up with any companies. If you're pursuing investment banking positions in New York City, well you may come up with a couple of hundred different company names. In my last job search I was pursuing a specific type of financial position within two regions, Massachusetts and Providence, RI. The total universe of companies I came up with was 120. You may be thinking that is a lot of names, and you're right, it is. But my list did not start out that large, rather it grew over time, and yours will as well. During the course of your job search you will likely become familiar with companies that either you've never heard of before, or companies that you have heard of, but did not know that the company housed the position that you're interested in pursuing.

Using my own prior job search as an example, the list of 120 companies I came up with, were sourced from the following:

1. **Prior business engagements.** These were companies I had done business with while working at the Federal government. This yielded ~10% of the companies on my target list.
2. **Linkedin.** The website provided me ~50% of the companies on my target list, far more than any other resource.
3. **Referrals.** This source was somewhat of a welcomed surprise. Often, what would happen is that during my networking meetings the person I was meeting with would say, "Have you heard of Company X?" or "I think Company X may be hiring." This method accounted for roughly 20% of the companies on my target list. The problem is sourcing companies through referrals is somewhat by chance, meaning you can't count on this method as your primary, or even secondary, source.
4. **Professional groups.** During my job search, as discussed earlier, I joined one industry trade group, the BSAS. By scouring the organization's member database, I was able to source roughly 20% of the companies on my target list.

Developing and writing out your target company list is required under my guidelines, it's not a recommendation. This can be a timely process, but it is not a terribly challenging exercise either. Developing my initial target list (remember your list will evolve overtime) was done over a weekend (~4 hours total was spent on this exercise). The list will keep you focused, save you time, and will assist you in establishing daily goals.

Once you have developed your raw list of company names it's helpful to input all of these names into a spreadsheet, and sort them by category. For instance, let's say you're pursuing a position in customer service within the healthcare industry. The "healthcare industry" is a large category, and too broad in my opinion to categorize all positions under a single umbrella. Therefore it would be best to break down the healthcare industry into smaller sub-categories, such as medical devices, pharmaceuticals, insurance, biotech, and hospital management (See Exhibit 1).

Exhibit 1. Company list for a candidate seeking a customer service role in healthcare

	Medical device companies	Pharmaceutical companies	Insurance companies	Biotech companies	Hospital mangmnt companies
1	Jones & Co.	Rick's pharma	XBC company	Kelly biotech	ABC Company
2	Smith & Co.		Blue Mountain		HMY Company
3					Mike's hospital management
4					

You can develop your own template for categorizing your companies, but the template I've shown in Exhibit 1 worked quite well for me.

Step 1: Using Linkedin to source target companies

Let's start generating that target company list, shall we? You'll need to login in to your Linkedin account and navigate to "advanced search". From here you will need to input your geographic region and then some key search words. For instance during my 2012 job search I would input the Boston zip code of 02210, set the location zone to within a 75 mile radius, and enter some short phrases in the keyword block. Keep the keyword phrases short, and specific. For instance writing the word "finance" or "healthcare" in the keyword search block is too generic, and is going to give you a list of individuals and companies that are likely to go well beyond your target universe. I recommend doing multiple searches with small phrases rather than one search with a long phrase. I had roughly ten short search phrases that I used when developing my target company list. These search phrases were often no more than a few words, and each phrase clearly distinguished the job I was seeking. The search phrase may be specific to a particular industry, or even better, specific to both an industry and job. For example a research analyst may use the phrase ["fixed income" "research analyst" energy]. Using this phrase is ideal because the job searcher is narrowing down the specific job they are seeking (research analyst) and job function (research within the energy sector). Moreover, the specific industry can be inferred from the term "fixed income", which is very specific to investment management.

One other function to be aware of when conducting searches is the use of quotes (" ") in the keyword block. To describe the function of quotes in the context of a search engine I will use an example. I would often use the quoted phrase "project finance" in my own Linkedin searches. If I did not quote the phrase, the search engine will simply look for any profile containing the word "project" and the word "finance", yet the two terms would not necessarily have to be sequential, or even appear in the same sentence or paragraph. Let me illustrate below.

Example 1.
Keyword search: "project finance".
Results: excerpt from Mike Jones's Profile
- Worked in the **Project Finance** division at the National Bank of the West from 2000-2005.

Example 2.
Keyword search: project finance (note no quotes this time).
Results: excerpt from Fred Jackson's Profile
- Worked on numerous coding **project**s while at Viper Data Inc. from 1996-2007
- Studied **Finance** at St. Harry's University

As you you can see from examples 1&2, the search results are very much different depending on how the key word is applied. When I conducted my search it was essential that the two terms (project and finance) be one continuous phrase, and therefore using the quotes was essential. By using the quotes around your phrase, the search engine will return profiles which contain the phrase exactly as you have written it. Another technique I frequently used was combining a quoted phrase, with one additional word. An example of this would be:

"project finance" energy

Regardless if the single word trails or follows the phrase in quotes, the results would be exactly the same. Therefore the preceding phrase could have also been written as:

energy "project finance"

This search will return all profiles that contain the phrase "project finance" and also contain the word "energy". You can put quotes around the word energy however it is not necessary simply because it is a single word, quotes are only necessary for phrases. Combining unique phrases and well selected words will help eliminate superfluous profiles from your search. Once you enter your phrase in the keyword block hit search and look at the results. You will likely see 10+ pages of Linkedin member profiles returned. These results will also reflect the employers of each of the members whose profiles were returned in the search, which is what we're really focused on in this exercise. Be aware that your search phrase may appear anywhere in that Linkedin member's profile. Meaning your search phrase could be related to that individual's current job or a prior job. The only way you'll really know if your phrase relates to an individual's current or prior employer is to click on the person's profile and do some reading. To explain this further, let's use an example. Suppose your search phrase is *"auto mechanic"*. You may see a profile returned which looks like:

John Smith
Manager at The Gap Companies

Now you're probably scratching your head wondering why the search is returning a profile of someone who works at The Gap when you're searching for auto mechanic profiles. The reason is if you click into John Smith's profile, you will likely find that he was an auto mechanic at some point in the past, but the only way to discover this is to click into the person's profile. Even if John Smith is not an auto-mechanic at this point in his career, the search is still successful. This is because you're more concerned with compiling company names, and John Smith's previous employer from when he was a mechanic could be your future employer.

Now if you're from the same region in which your search is focused you may be familiar with a number of the company names you see, and it will quickly become apparent that those companies would likely offer the position you are seeking. If this is the case, great, start adding those company names to your spreadsheet. If however you start seeing companies in your search that you are unfamiliar with, then don't immediately add those companies to your list, do a little digging first. Click into the individual's profile. Read a description of the work the individual performed while at the company. Is it what you are looking for or is it a red herring? I will give you an example of a red herring. As I stated earlier one of the search phrases I utilized was *"project finance"*. Project Finance for those of you who are unfamiliar with the term literally means the act of financing a project. That "project" would typically relate to an energy development (e.g., gas fired power plant, wind farm, nuclear plant, etc.) or an infrastructure project (e.g., bridge, toll roads, airport, etc). However occasionally I would run the search and come across a company name I was unfamiliar with. I would then proceed to take a peek at the individual's profile, and low and behold the way in which the individual was using the phrase "project finance" to describe their job was in a completely different context than what I was expecting. I would occasionally find a profile in which the Linkedin member was referring to an IT (information technology) project that they helped finance, which was completely unrelated to the "project finance" profiles I was seeking.

If you think your search may be tainted by a common red herring there is a very simple solution. Let's use my last example. If I want to avoid technology related project finance profiles I would type in the search block ["project finance" -technology]. By including the "-" in front of the word technology the search will exclude any profiles that include the word technology.

You've been warned, don't start immediately writing down company names unless you are sure that the company in question is not a red herring! Now that you have the basic tools necessary to start searching, you should take Linkedin for a test drive. The more searches you do with words and phrases, the more creative you will become, and the more focused your search results will be. Conducting searches is no different than any other activity you undertake, practice goes a long way.

Step 2. Finding the right people to network with

Before taking the next step you should have accumulated an orderly list of companies that you believe house positions that you are seeking. Now whether or not the company is currently hiring for the position you're interested in is irrelevant, you still need to be speaking with people at these companies. It's absolutely critical you not solely focus on companies that have job openings because the reality is, the universe of companies that may be hiring at this moment in time, could be small in scope.

The next step in our journey is identifying specific individuals to network with. So who exactly should you choose to reach out to? After all, some of these companies on your list may have thousands of employees. It's best you focus your efforts on those individuals that are most likely to respond to your inquiry and, more importantly, can assist you in your search. In an ideal world the individuals you network with should meet most of the following criteria:

1. **Currently working in the position you are seeking, or at a minimum, working in a division of the company which houses your target position.** If you are seeking a mechanical engineering job at Boeing, you should be speaking with other mechanical engineers at Boeing, not for instance someone in Boeing's marketing division.

2. **At your career level or above.** My rule of thumb is to reach out to individuals at your career level or higher. You are likely to have the most in common, on many levels, with individuals at your own career level, thus making the conversation easier. I would not reach out to individuals that are well below you're career level because their ability to assist you may be limited. Furthermore, individuals below your career level may have a lack of understanding as it relates to the position you're seeking.

3. **Went to the same high school, college, or graduate school as you.** I have found over the years that networking response rates exponentially increase if the job seeker and the person they are networking with have the same alma mater in common. Although alumnus from all levels of education tend to be responsive to networking inquiries, it seems logical that one would find the greatest number of networking opportunities with classmates from their highest level of education.

4. **Individuals on LinkedIn with many connections (say greater than 200).** People with a greater number of connections are more likely to be frequent users of LinkedIn, and will in turn, be more likely to respond to your inquiry. Simply click into the individual's LinkedIn profile and see how many people they are connected with (the number of connections will appear just to the right of their name). Not to mention, those people who have many connections are more likely to be able to introduce you to someone that could further you along in your search.

5. **Have a mutual connection to the individual you are networking with.** A mutual connection could include a friend, colleague, or classmate. If you have a mutual connection with the person you are trying to network with the chances of receiving a response from that individual goes up dramatically. Next to each individual's name that is returned in a LinkedIn search there will appear a number (1st, 2nd, or 3rd) indicating how closely you are connected to that individual. A "2nd" implies that you and the individual in the search have a direct mutual connection. You may want to consider asking your mutual connection for an introduction to the person you are trying to network with, this will certainly increase the likelihood of a response.

You must also be cognizant of the potential situation that if you attempt to network with someone that is a mutual connection to one of your colleagues, your colleague may come to find out you are job searching. Perhaps this doesn't bother you, but perhaps it does. Either way, it's important you're aware of the risk.

Criteria number 1 on the aforementioned list is by far the most important. In fact, if the individual you plan to network with doesn't at least meet criteria number 1, then I would strongly consider passing on that individual, unless it's a unique circumstance. The beauty of Linkedin is that you can conduct searches for all the criteria listed above. Once you identify a potential individual you would like to network with, get to work.

A Case Study in Networking

The following case study illustrates, from start to finish, how to effectively identify and pursue a networking candidate.

> Rosco Hawk is a marketing professional searching for a job in Boston, MA. Rosco is currently working in the sports division of a Chicago based marketing firm called Horizon Marketing. Rosco focuses on the marketing of athletic apparel. His expertise is advertising campaigns for live athletic events typically held in a stadium or some other athletic arena. Rosco is pursuing a job which falls within his core area of expertise. He logs into his Linkedin account and through some advanced searches he identifies a man named Dirk McDougal. Dirk works for Ultimate Apparel, a manufacturer of athletic equipment and apparel, and is located just outside of Boston. Dirk's Linkedin profile reveals he is a Vice President in Ultimate Apparel's marketing division. He does not work in the live athletic events marketing division as Rosco does at Horizon, but rather Dirk's expertise is in digital media advertising. Although Dirk is not performing the precise job that Rosco is seeking, he does work in the marketing division. Dirk has been employed with Ultimate Apparel for seven years and therefore likely has many contacts in the marketing division (his Linkedin profile also shows he has 304 connections). Furthermore, Rosco and Dirk both attended Eastern Wolverine College (they graduated in different classes, and do not know each other).

On a scale of "1 to 10", with "10" being the most ideal person Rosco should network with, I would score Dirk a "7" (not too bad). I deducted some points because Dirk is not working in the position Rosco is pursuing, but given that he works in the same division, has a solid network of contacts, and the two attended the same college (which greatly increases the chances that Dirk will respond to Rosco's inquiry), Rosco should undoubtedly reach out to Dirk.

Once Rosco decides to reach out to Dirk, he drafts the following note which he will send through "InMail" (InMail, as a reminder, is LinkedIn's version of email).

> *Dirk,*
>
> *Let me take this time to introduce myself, my name is Rosco Hawk. I came across your profile on LinkedIn because of your affiliation with Eastern Wolverine College, and your role with Ultimate Apparel.*
>
> *For the past three years I have been a Vice President in the creative development division for Horizon Marketing in Chicago. My division is primarily focused on creative development for billboard marketing campaigns at live sporting events. Since joining the creative development division I have worked on marketing campaigns for Nike, Under Armour, and Asics, among others.*
>
> *I am currently pursuing new career opportunities in the Boston area, with a focus on footwear and athletic apparel marketing. I would welcome the opportunity to speak with you about Ultimate Apparel, and your role with the firm. Please let me know if you would have availability sometime this week.*
>
> *I appreciate your time and assistance.*
>
> *Rosco Hawk*
> *555-689-1212*

What you see in the example above is the same general template that I have used literally hundreds of times. It's informative, and more important, to the point. If you noticed, I mention the Eastern Wolverine College connection early in the email, which should spark some interest, and motivate Dirk to keep reading. If you have any connection to the person you are reaching out to, mention the connection in the first or second sentence of the email. If you have no connection to the person you are reaching out to, that's perfectly fine, however you should mention in the first or second sentence how you came across that individual's profile, and why you are interested in speaking with that person. It could be as simple as stating "I came across your profile on LinkedIn because of your role in global digital marketing with Ultimate Apparel." Also, notice in the last sentence I infer that the conversation should take place this week as opposed to leaving the date of the conversation open ended. Rosco also could have chosen to conclude his letter by saying, "It would be great if we could try to grab a coffee next time I'm in Boston". I would only suggest that Rosco go down that route if he absolutely knew he was going to be in Boston within the next two or three weeks. It's always best to meet with someone in person, but this may prove difficult for Rosco given that he lives in Chicago and seeking a job in Boston. When I was job searching for a position in Boston, but living in Washington DC, I was back in Boston frequently, so I had the luxury of setting up face to face meetings. That said, I also had to do a great deal of networking over the phone.

Now if Dirk responds to Rosco's inquiry, that's great (I'll discuss next steps in a moment), but what if he doesn't? My rule of thumb is to always send at least one other email if you don't get a response to your initial email. In the midst of my own adventures in networking, it was not uncommon that I received no response to my initial email, but did receive a response to my follow up email. Common reasons why someone may not respond to your initial email include the recipient simply forgetting to respond, or the email getting lost in the shuffle of the recipient's inbox. Some individuals, myself included, get over one-hundred emails per day, so it's not surprising if one or more emails gets deleted or overlooked by accident. Now if you sent an "InMail" through LinkedIn and the recipient doesn't respond, well you may be out of luck, because you don't want to waste two InMails on one individual when you're only allowed three InMails per month (you can of course have access to more Inmails, you'll simply pay a higher monthly subscription fee to LinkedIn). The bottom line here is if you sent a networking candidate an email, and they don't initially respond, then definitely follow up. I recommend forwarding the original email with a short note attach. Here is an example:

> *Dirk,*
>
> *I want to make sure you received the attached email I sent to you last week. Please respond when you have a moment.*
>
> *Thanks again,*
> *Rosco*

The follow up email is as simple as that. As inferred from the note, Dirk has appropriately attached his initial email to the follow up email.

What you absolutely don't want to do is send out a networking email and then sit on your hands waiting for a response. I've received responses to networking emails literally months after I sent them. Now of course that is an extreme example, but it does happen. If the recipient chooses to respond to your networking inquiry, they will usually do so within a week or less based on my experience. Ideally you want to be having a networking call, or meeting, every few days. So in order to keep that pace, you need to be sending out networking introduction emails constantly. When I was in core job searching mode I would send out on average five emails a week. The responses will come back on a rolling basis, which will align nicely with your target of one networking call every few days.

If Rosco receives no response from Dirk after a second attempt in reaching out to him, then unfortunately Rosco needs to cut his losses and move on. This can be a frustrating situation that you may encounter, especially if you believe the person you're reaching out to can be an asset to your job search. The reality is though that not every single person is going be to receptive to your inquiries. The response rate will be high if you strategically target a certain audience using my guidelines, but it's unlikely to be 100%.

Now let's assume Dirk is receptive to Rosco's initial, or second email. Dirk's response will most likely be something along the lines of:

> *Rosco,*
>
> *Thanks for reaching out. I'd be happy to chat, give me a call when you have a chance.*
>
> *Dirk*
> *781.888.9999*

Dirk's response to Rosco's email is the same response that I received many times during my adventures in networking. One thing I have learned over the years is to never call someone at a random time, even if they suggest you do so, as Dirk has done in his response to Rosco. I always recommend establishing a specific time prior to speaking with your networking counterpart. There are so many reasons for doing so and I will discuss a few.

Let's assume for a moment that Rosco picks up the phone and calls Dirk at 11:18 am on a Monday (random date/time). Dirk answers, and is willing to talk, but has a meeting he must attend at 11:30am. This is a situation you want to avoid. There is nothing worse than a few minutes into a networking call the person on the other end of the line says, "I only have another five minutes." Now you could set up another call to continue the discussion, but that's not ideal. You don't want to drag this whole thing out longer than it needs to be. You want to have one call, get your message across, and then move on to the next networking target. Let's consider a second situation where Rosco calls Dirk at a random time during the day. Assume Dirk does not answer the phone and Rosco leaves a voicemail. This situation could end in a vicious cycle of phone-tag, with both parties getting frustrated, and everyone's time is wasted. To avoid the situations I have described takes very little effort. You simply need to set up a specific time to talk. Rosco should respond to Dirk's email with the following brief response:

Dirk,

Thank you for responding to my email. Would you be available to speak this Wednesday at 1pm? If so, I will call you at the number you provided.

Regards,
Rosco

Ideally you want to limit the number of emails that are traded back and forth, so always be pushing the agenda forward. For instance, you can see in the last email Rosco appropriately suggested a date and time, rather than simply asking Dirk what time works for him.

Now let's assume Dirk responds that he is indeed available on that date and time, and looks forward to speaking with Rosco. Don't start sweating bullets if you're in Rosco's situation, but it looks like this conversation is a go. Congrats to Rosco for securing what could be a very productive networking call.

Rosco must now start preparing for his networking call with Dirk. Please do not show up for any networking call, or meeting, unprepared. It's an amateur mistake, so avoid it. I would typically spend, on average, an hour preparing for each networking call or meeting. The first time you prepare for a networking call it may in fact take much longer, but your prep time will get quicker with repetition.

There are three goals you should set out to accomplish with each networking call/meeting, and it is these goals that will guide your preparation. Goal #1: Explain what you do in your current role; Goal #2: Ask well thought out questions about the individual's company and division; Goal #3: Have an endgame in mind, then complete it.

Now Rosco requested the call, which also means he will be controlling the direction and pace of the call, as will you. So here is a little secret, you can script the call in advance, exactly as you see fit. The call is a blank slate, and now you have become the author. This is a strategy that I have used countless times over the years, and it works flawlessly. Like anything else in life, the more you do it, the better you will become at it.

When I say, "script the call in advance", I literally mean you need to write out the conversation in advance on your computer. I know this tactic may come across as odd, but I assure you it works. Here's what Rosco should draft in advance of the call:

> *Hi Dirk, This is Rosco Hawk calling. How are you doing today? Thank you once again for taking the time out of your schedule to chat, I appreciate it. As I mentioned in my email, I came across your profile on LinkedIn because of your role with Ultimate Apparel and because of your affiliation with Eastern Wolverine College. I also thought you may be a good person to speak with that could share some insight into Ultimate Apparel and, more specifically, its marketing division.*

> *Now I did have a few questions I would like to run by you, but I thought it may be helpful if I first gave you some background information on myself and my role with Horizon Marketing, if that sounds good. (the person on the other end of the line will almost always say "sure, that would be great" or something to that affect)*

> *Well I joined Horizon in 2009, and was recently promoted to Vice President in our live events division. I'm not sure how familiar you are with Horizon, but the company focuses on the retail consumer with a specialization in the marketing of sports apparel and athletic footwear. We've been fortunate enough to work with most of the major sporting labels including Adidas, Bauer, and Under Armour. My division works directly with both athletic apparel companies as well as sporting arenas across North America where we can roll out our marketing programs.*

> *In my role, I act as a relationship manager, and am the primary point of contact between the client and our firm. I conduct the initial kickoff meeting with new clients, and work with them in developing a marketing theme for the product they are rolling out. I'm also in charge of identifying sporting arenas across the country that would be ideal for displaying Horizon's customers' advertising campaigns. Additionally, I'm in charge of negotiating contract*

terms with the sporting arenas on behalf of out apparel clients.
Finally, I work closely with our artists, our attorneys, the client's
marketing team, as well as the arena's corporate development team.

I think that's a good overview of Horizon and my role with the firm,
but if you have any questions I'd be happy to answer them,
otherwise I can jump right into some of the questions I have for you.
(if the person on the other end of the line asks some follow up
questions, they will rarely be difficult, most likely general questions
about your firm or role).

Next is your opportunity to ask the person on the other end of the line some insightful questions. I recommend asking 3-5 questions, that's the sweet spot. Your questions should be thoughtful, but not overly complex. Here are the questions Rosco asks Dirk:

1. *First, I was hoping you could provide a general overview of the marketing division at Ultimate Apparel, specifically I'm trying to get a feel for the structure of the division and how it is organized?*
2. *Could you describe who you're interacting with in your role, either internally or outside of the company?*
3. *You've been with the company for a few years now so perhaps you could elaborate on how the work has evolved with changes in consumer tastes? Similarly, how has your work evolved with the introduction of advertising via social media and other digital forums?*
4. *What are some of the challenges that Ultimate Apparel's marketing division has faced over the past year?*

As you can see, the questions are brief, not too difficult (but thoughtful), and should really give you a better perspective on the company and division which you hope to work for some day. Remember when asking your questions be respectful of your networking counterpart's privacy. There is a fine line between asking insightful questions and digging too deep into the company's affairs. I don't suggest having more than five questions planned because the responses that your questions elicit will often prompt further questions. Between the questions you have prepared, and the questions that will naturally arise on the call, there will be plenty to discuss.

Something I want to emphasize is that you need to get a notebook specifically for your networking calls. I can't express how important it is to get in the habit of writing down the questions you ask, and the answers you receive during each call. This will come in handy, and I will discuss why later.

The last part of the conversation is the closing, and should be considered the most important part of the call. With every call you engage in you should have an endgame in mind, and the closing is the spot to make sure that endgame is achieved. When I was doing networking calls my endgame may have included any of the following -   simply making a good first impression, securing an introduction to someone else I could network with (which is Rosco's goal), sending the person my resume to submit on my behalf, or securing a face to face meeting. I can't tell you exactly what your endgame should be, but you should certainly have one.   Moreover, accomplishing your endgame should place you in a stronger position than you were in prior to the call.   Without a goal in mind, you may be left questioning whether the call was worth your while.

Let's pickup our conversation as Rosco delivers his close.

> *Well Dirk, I don't have any other questions for you today, but this was all very informative for me. As I mentioned at the beginning of our call, I'm interested in pursuing marketing opportunities in Ultimate Apparel's live events group. If you happen to have any contacts in that group, I would certainly welcome an introduction.*

At this point, based on my experience Dirk will likely say something along the lines of, "Sure, let me give it some thought, and I can probably come up with a name or two".

No matter what your endgame is you should always end the call by leaving the lines of communication open. As an example, Rosco may say, "If it's ok with you Dirk, I'd like to touch base every couple of months, in case you happen to hear of any opportunities that may come across your desk." You can come up with your own line, but make sure the underlying theme is that you will be staying in touch.

Well hats off to Rosco, he's completed his first networking call. As I said earlier, I've done a ton of these calls over the years. You would be surprised how similar each call is once you get into a rhythm. As I said earlier, you are requesting the call and therefore you are also given the opportunity to direct the course of the conversation. There will however be times in which your call doesn't go by the script. Occasionally during my adventures in networking, a caller would flip the table and start asking me challenging questions, as if I were on an interview. Don't worry, this happens very infrequently. Most networking calls feel as if you are having a casual conversation with a friend about work. The last point I will make is you shouldn't feel obligated to go by *my* script. You should write a script that sounds natural to you, and natural to the way you talk. I'm sure this goes without saying, but practice your script aloud before you jump on the call to make sure it flows.

Once you're done with a call there are two more steps you must take before you can call it a day and pour yourself a glass of Caol Ila (my favorite single malt scotch). First, you need to fill in your call log (see Exhibit 2). This step is an important task which you must incorporate into your day to day activities.

Exhibit 2. Sample call log

Name	Company	Division	Origin	Date of initial inquiry	Date of initial call	Date of follow-ups	Notes
Dirk M.	Ultimate Apparel	Digital Marketing	Linkedin	Dec. 26	1.3.16		Dirk stated he would make an introduction to someone in the live events marketing group. Follow-up with him in 2-3 weeks.

A call log will come in handy for keeping track of those contacts who you've reached out to, those you've actually spoken with, and those which require follow-ups. During my job search in 2013 I reached out to over 100 individuals over the course of 9 months. Now there is no way I would be able to remember the context of each of those calls unless I kept a call log.

Every two weeks I would do a scan of my call log. I would highlight a row "red" in the log if I had not spoken with that individual in more than six weeks. The red signal reminded me that I needed to "follow-up" with that individual as soon as time permitted (we'll dive into the subject of follow-ups shortly).

The final task you need to perform is to send your contact a quick thank you note (within 48 hours of the call). It should be brief. Here is an example.

> *Dirk,*
>
> *Thanks again for taking the time to speak with me yesterday. I found the conversation to be informative, particularly your insight into branding within the context of social media. As I indicated on our call I would be interested in speaking with your colleague in live events marketing, and I appreciate your offer to make an introduction.*
>
> *Have a great weekend,*
>
> *Rosco*

Finally, Rosco's job is done, right? Well, for the moment, yes. But what if a week goes by and Rosco has heard nothing from Dirk? The correct answer is that Rosco needs to follow-up with his networking counterpart. The act of "following-up" is worthy of some attention. There are two situations in which one needs to follow-up. The first is the very situation Rosco may find himself in, where Dirk has committed to doing something for Rosco, but after a week Rosco has heard nothing from him. The reality is this is an extremely common situation, and one in which Rosco should not take personally. There are a variety of reasons why Dirk has not followed up with Rosco, and it's likely that none of those reasons have anything to do with Dirk's feelings towards Rosco. Dirk has willingly agreed to introduce Rosco to a colleague in live events marketing, and therefore if Rosco has not heard back from Dirk within ten business days, then he has every right to follow-up with him.

The follow-up email should be brief and to the point. Dirk may have very well intended to reach out to a colleague on behalf of Rosco, however something could have distracted him at work, at home, or he simply just forgot. A follow-up email from Rosco after a week shows Dirk that Rosco is serious about speaking with someone else at Ultimate Apparel, and it displays his commitment in securing a new job. In Rosco's case, the follow-up email should look something like this:

Hi Dirk,

Hope all is well. When we spoke a couple of weeks ago you indicated that you'd be willing to put me in touch with your colleague in events marketing. I'm still interested in taking you up on that offer. When you have a moment it would be great if you could pass along his contact information.

Sincerely,
Rosco

There is a high probability Dirk will respond to Rosco at this point. However, there is also the possibility he doesn't respond, and I've been in this exact situation. During my job search in 2012 I had, what I thought, was a very good face-to-face networking meeting. The individual I met with offered (on his own accord) to put me in touch with an industry contact of his, but after the meeting I never heard from him again. I sent two follow-up emails to this individual, and never received a response. It was a terrible feeling, and I couldn't help but think that I did something wrong during our encounter. The reality is something like what I just described may very well happen to you during your job search. It's a terrible feeling, but you need to move forward and cut your losses. I think knowing that a situation like this may occur may actually make the sting a bit less painful if/when it happens. Fortunately it happens infrequently. Out of the 100+ people I reached out to in my last job search I can only recall one instance where someone agreed to make an introduction and did not follow through on their word.

Now there is a second scenario which requires "following-up" and it's as important as the scenario we just went through, so pay attention! Let's assume for a minute that Dirk introduces Rosco to his colleague, Brian Rock. Brian Rock and Rosco have a networking call and it goes well. Let's also assume that the networking encounter ends with Brian stating that he would alert Rosco if any job opportunities surfaced at Ultimate Apparel that met Rosco's qualifications and interests. By the way, that is how 75% of your networking calls or networking meetings will end. Now Rosco may be thinking to himself, "Brian said he will follow-up with me when a job opens up at Ultimate Apparel, so I'll wait to hear from him." That sounds reasonable on the surface, and that's what you would hope would happen, but it's not the appropriate strategy Rosco should be taking. As a job seeker, Rosco in essence is a salesman. He of course is selling himself. Now I know we all don't have a salesman type mentality (myself included), but the reality is that as job seekers, that is exactly what we have become, whether we like it or not. That said, Rosco must stay aggressive, just as a salesman would.   Let me be very clear here, there is a clear distinction between aggressive and annoying behavior. The challenge for you as the job seeker is to remain aggressive, without becoming a pest.

To understand the importance of "following-up" you need to place yourself in the shoes of the person who you reached out to. It could be 3, 6, or 9 months before Brian Rock comes across a position that matches Rosco's qualifications. At that point, Brian may have simply forgotten about Rosco. Perhaps Brian incorrectly assumes Rosco already found a new position, or perhaps Brian incorrectly assumes that Rosco has not reached back out to him because he really isn't all that interested in his company. Job seekers, particularly those on the verge of finishing school, frequently reach out to me to network. I always make time to speak with these individuals. The reality though is that I speak with so many people that I tend to forget who I've spoken with, and their situation. The unfortunate thing is very few individuals actually follow-up with me, and as a result, they're forgotten. It's the old adage, "Out of sight, out of mind." By following-up with Brian on a regular basis, Rosco will stay fresh in his head, and when a job does surface, hopefully Rosco will be the first to get alerted. The good news is following up simply requires a quick email, not another call (although you could request another call if you're so inclined).   The effort required is minimal, and the dividends can be huge.

Here is an example of a follow-up email, which I recommend sending to your contacts every 6-8 weeks.

> *Brian,*
>
> *It's been a couple of months since we last spoke so I thought I would send you a quick email to check-in. Work is going well on my end. Most recently I'm working with a global athletic footwear manufacturer for a new cleated shoe the company has coming to market next month. In conjunction with the product's release, I'm developing a promo event for the Australian Rugby tournament next month.*
>
> *I remain interested in hearing about any opportunities in events marketing at Ultimate Apparel and would appreciate it if you kept me in mind if anything comes across your desk.*
>
> *Have a great summer, and I'll speak with you soon.*
>
> *Rosco*

That's it, simple and to the point. I'll tell you right now that if I had not done my follow-ups during my last job search, I'd not be in the position I am today. In fact, I followed-up with the individual who referred me to my current position a total of three times over a six month period. My follow-ups were brief, friendly, informative, and most important, not annoying or pushy. I can also say with certainty that had I not followed-up with the person who referred me to my job, he would have forgotten about me. I hate to be the bearer of bad news, but on a scale of importance to the people you network with, you fall on a level that is far below lunch plans for the day. The point here is, it becomes very easy for Brian to forget about people like Rosco, especially after long periods of time. Rosco needs to stay fresh in the minds of all the people he is speaking with, and so do you. This is one of the most important concepts in this book.

Chapter 4: Searching and applying for jobs online

Let me say right off the bat that I am a bit prejudice against using online job postings as a primary method for sourcing potential jobs. Every job I've ever had since graduating college, that would be six in total for those of you counting, has come through networking. Now that doesn't mean I didn't apply for jobs online along the way, of course I did. In fact I applied to many jobs online, just with little success. Let me throw some numbers at you – during my job search of 2012 I applied to fifty-four jobs over a nine month period. Fifty one of those jobs were sourced through online job searching activities while the remainder were sourced through networking. Out of the fifty one jobs that I sourced through job boards, only one converted into an actual interview (an interview hit rate of ~2%). However, out of the three jobs I sourced through networking, all led to an interview, and one of those interviews yielded an offer (an interview hit rate of 100%). I think the numbers speak for themselves. It's clear that job opportunities sourced through networking come along far less frequently than job opportunities sourced through non-networking methods, but when they do come along, the probability of securing an interview is far superior.

Over the years I have drawn a few conclusions about online job searching. The first conclusion is that scouring the internet, and applying to unsolicited jobs (i.e. job opportunities to which you have no strategic relationship with the company), will rarely deliver the results you are seeking. However, online job searching is somewhat of a necessary evil, like buying a car. The good news is that there are techniques you can use to improve the likelihood that your efforts will at least yield a call back from the prospective company.

My first piece of advice is to stay far clear from Monster, Careerbuilder, Hotjobs, or any other job board that is marketed to the masses. Recruiters that post to these sites are far more interested in making placements than your career interests. Let me give you an example. Now I would consider myself to have a well constructed resume, detailing my career interests and background. However, the only calls I ever received as a result of having my resume posted to Monster and Careerbuilder were from recruiters trying to pitch me on sales jobs which had absolutely no correlation to my background or interests. That became incredibly frustrating and annoying after a while. Picture this, it's 2012, I'm doing energy banking with the U.S. government, I have two masters degree, and am a level 3 CFA candidate, and I get a call from a recruiter who found my resume on Monster asking me if I'm interested in selling life insurance with a national insurer. Let me be clear, I have nothing against a career in selling insurance. The point is, selling life insurance had absolutely nothing to do with my career interests, nor my prior work experience. I had been working in the energy sector for four years, why all of the sudden would I want to sell life insurance? Now I just described one incident in which a recruiter tried to pitch me a random job, but this type of situation would happen all the time. Low and behold, these recruiters would all source my contact information from the mass marketed job boards.

Moreover, consider that mass marketed job boards are just that, job boards that cater to the MASSES. Don't be one of many in the herd pursuing the same highly marketed position. If you find an attractive position on one of these websites I can assure you that many others have found it too. You will likely be one of hundreds applying to the same job, particularly if the position is in a major metro city. Simply due to the sheer number of resumes received, the company posting the job may not have the adequate resources, or the time, to appropriately review your resume. We need to make sure your resume gets into the appropriate hands and is given the review it rightly deserves.

My other gripe with big job boards like Monster or Careerbuilder is that these websites have become overly cluttered with articles, advertisements, and ancillary services (e.g., resume writing tools; interview resources; etc.), leaving the user scratching their head where to begin, and feeling overwhelmed. I want my job board site to be pure, avoiding any unnecessary clutter, similar to what google.com is to internet searches. The bottom line is, stay away from the big job board sites, these are the ones that are typically advertised on TV during a Super Bowl commercial and are also found on website banners, billboards, subways, or on the radio. I've said my peace, and I think you know where I stand on this topic.

Now that I've given my pitch on why you shouldn't spend your valuable time posting your resume on big job boards, let me explain how you still may be able to use certain job boards to your advantage. Simplyhired.com, Indeed.com, and LinkUp.com are worthy of a drop in from time to time. These sites have become known as "aggregators" because they aggregate jobs from various sites (e.g., other job boards, recruiter sites, company sites) to a single site. This is certainly more efficient from the job seeker's perspective as it eliminates the need to spend time hopping from site to site, and job board to job board. Out of the three aggregators I recommended, LinkUp.com is my favorite. The two issues I have come across with aggregators in general is that postings tend to become stale, and second, aggregators may pull the same position from multiple sources, which can cause duplicative postings. LinkUp.com seems to avoid these issues for the most part. Furthermore, the sites I recommended are quite simplistic, avoiding the information onslaught imposed by the big job boards. Although not an aggregator, and actually more inline with a traditional job board, Linkedin.com also offers job seekers the opportunity to search and apply for jobs through its site. Linkedin.com is the only traditional job board I recommend because of its ability to make the connection between companies, jobs, job seekers, and potential network opportunities.

To save yourself some time, consider the following. Rather than logging in daily to the sites I suggested, I recommend setting up pre-arranged searches that are emailed to you daily. These pre-arranged searches are set up using keywords (e.g., "electrical engineer") and a geographic focus (e.g., within 20 miles of Boston, MA). Every day, or however often you decide, emails will be sent to you with new jobs that have been posted based on your specific criteria. All of the sites I referenced earlier offer this feature. Regardless of the method you use to source jobs online, whether it be going directly to the job board, or having jobs emailed to you directly, if you do decide to apply for a job online, always, and I mean ALWAYS, attempt to reach out to someone of relevance at the company prior to applying. You will be in a far better strategic position if you can have someone at the company submit your resume rather than going through an online job portal. Moreover, it's in your best interest to speak with someone who is knowledgable about the job opening so you are completely informed about the position you're pursuing. However, if your attempts to speak with someone at the firm have only led to dead ends then you should certainly apply online before the position is removed from the job board.

For investment professionals read here!
For those of you in the investment community there is one job portal which I consider better than any of the sites I have mentioned thus far, and that portal is Bloomberg. The Bloomberg service (accessed through a community or personal terminal) is widely used in the investment sector, and provides real time investment data to finance professionals. Note: My references to "Bloomberg" are specifically related to the Bloomberg terminal service. Don't confuse a Bloomberg terminal with bloomberg.com, the two are very different. One day I happened to stumble upon Bloomberg's job board, and what a pleasant surprise it was. What makes Bloomberg's job board truly unique is that Bloomberg requires the poster of the job to leave their personal contact information. When I found this it was like striking gold. Traditionally when applying for a job online I'd ask myself, "is anyone reviewing this application, or is my application simply going into the dreaded black hole?" I'm sure many of you have felt the same way. With Bloomberg I knew the answer to that question because my application (resume and cover

letter) were emailed directly to the job poster. Additionally, by having a job poster's information, it allowed me to follow up with that individual and inquire about the status of the position in question. For those of you who may have access to a Bloomberg terminal, I strongly recommend you check out the job board. I think you'll be impressed with the quality, selectivity, and quantity of jobs posted. If you work in asset management, but don't have access to a Bloomberg terminal, consider asking a friend or contact in the industry, that may have access to a terminal, to conduct periodic searches on your behalf. You can access the Bloomberg job board through the function JOBS<GO>.

As a job searcher you need to get creative and constantly be thinking outside the box on methods to generate job leads. As an example, during my job search in 2012, I generated an abundance of leads through an industry trade group I joined called the Boston Security Analysts Society or BSAS. In addition to providing networking leads, as discussed earlier, the BSAS had a robust online job board specifically catered towards hiring investment professionals in the Boston area (my geographic focus). What I loved about the BSAS job board is that the contact information of the job poster was provided to the applicant. This allowed me to send my resume directly to the job poster via email, a superior advantage over those applicants who may be applying through other means. Moreover, most of the job postings were exclusive to the BSAS website. Therefore the applicant pool was far smaller than what would be expected on a free job board site, and this of course increases the likelihood of a call back. I know the readers of this book are seeking jobs in all different industries, so I can't say exactly which professional organizations would be most beneficial to you. The point is these organizations and industry specific trade groups are out there, you just need to do a little leg work to find them.

Now that you have compiled a list of companies which you'll be targeting, you should get in the habit of picking 3-5 companies each day from your list and venturing to those companies' job boards to see if new opportunities have been posted. It's not uncommon for an open position to show up exclusively on the company's own job board. The bottom line is you have to cover all your bases.

Another source of online job postings, which certainly cannot be discounted, are staffing agency websites. More often than not if you find a job you're interested in on a recruiter's site, the recruiter's contact information will be posted alongside the job. I strongly recommend following up with that recruiter once you have submitted your application.

The tactic I'm trying to instill here is that you need to be looking where others are not. Exclusivity is your friend.

Chapter 5: Desperate times

At some point during your job search you may begin to feel a sense of desperation. I certainly did during my last job search. After about six months of busting my hump trying to make things happen, I felt utterly disappointed and somewhat defeated from the lack of opportunities that had come my way. The harder I tried the more it felt as if I was running in place. I was desperate for something to happen that would give me a sense of progress in my search. So what's a job seeker to do once that feeling of despair sets in? What shouldn't a job seeker do once desperation sets in? These are all natural questions to ask, and important to have answered.

As I said earlier, I began having these desperate feelings about six months into my job search, and although six months certainly feels like a long time in the moment, it's really not. In January of 2011 (one and a half years after the end of the Great Financial Recession[8], there were still 6.2 million Americans that had been unemployed for more than 27 weeks[9] (6.5+ months). Another statistic to put this all in perspective is that by January 2011 the average duration of unemployment for an individual in the United Stated (i.e. has actively looked for work in the prior four weeks) was 37 weeks[10] or roughly 9 months. The point I'm trying to drive home here is that although you may get frustrated after a few months of job searching, you won't get much sympathy from the large majority of job seekers in this era we're living in. So take a step back, and try to keep the duration of your search in perspective.

You should go into a job search expecting it will take 6-9 months to land a job. However, if the United States reaches normal unemployment levels, which the Federal Reserve considers to be in the 4.6-5%[11] range, expect this time frame to tighten. This means upon entering a job search you should be

---

[8] The National Bureau of Economic Research. "Business Cycle Dating Committee" <http://www.nber.org/cycles/sept2010.html>

[9] Bureau of Labor Statistics. "Number unemployed for 27 weeks & Over" <http://data.bls.gov/cgi-bin/surveymost?ln>

[10]Bureau of Labor Statistics. "Average weeks unemployed" <http://data.bls.gov/cgi-bin/surveymost?ln>

[11] Board of Governors of the Federal Reserve System. "What is the lowest level of unemployment that the U.S. economy can sustain?" <http://www.federalreserve.gov/faqs/economy_14424.htm>

mentally prepared to go to battle for an extended period. Consider yourself to be embarking upon a marathon. There is of course certainly the chance that you may find yourself nine months into a job search with no light at the end of the tunnel. Note that during the months of November and December, job searching activities come to a slow grind due to holidays in the United States. If you're job searching during these months, expect minimal activity. From my experience, job hiring is most active in the first half of the year, immediately after corporate budgets are established and bonuses are paid.

At this point you should be quite certain about the job you are pursuing. With that in mind it's important to not get tempted, particularly during bouts of desperation, by every single job that may meet one or more of your requirements. Similarly, don't get lured into applying to every job for which you are qualified. An example from my own adventures in job searching may be beneficial here.

About three months into my last job search I was becoming frustrated at the lack of success I was having. One day in my daily search I came across a posting on a staffing agency's website for a position with an energy company in Massachusetts. The position looked somewhat interesting and I knew based on the job description and the required qualifications that I was well suited for the role. I picked up the phone, called the recruiter, and followed up by sending my resume to her. About a week later I received a call back from the recruiter informing me that the company liked my resume and wanted to have a phone interview. Of course I was excited to finally get some interest in my resume from a potential employer, but I wasn't as excited as I should have been. After some soul searching I came to a realization. Although the job was interesting, the company was solid, and I was qualified for the role, the position itself was not really in line with my long term career objectives.

Now I found myself in this odd position where I had to prepare for an interview for a job that was of little interest to me. Sure I could have cancelled the interview, but I decided not to. For one, if I cancelled the interview the recruiter probably wouldn't have worked with me again, and two, I needed to get some job interviewing under my belt. Like anything else, the more you practice something the better you become at it. At the end of the day I prepared for the interview as I would any other, and had a call with the HR manager from the company. I didn't get a call back for a second interview and believe me I wasn't all that bent out of shape about it. Although I spent a good amount of time preparing for an interview when I could have been focusing my efforts elsewhere, I learned a valuable lesson. The lesson was that I needed to stay focused in my search. I knew exactly what I wanted, and I needed to stay committed to that goal. Unless you are in a very desperate situation, I suggest you too stay committed to your initial goal. As we discussed earlier in the book, before jumping into a search you need to sit down and determine what exactly it is you want to achieve in your next position. Of course your interests may drift slightly during your search, but having a core target in mind will prevent you from pursuing peripheral jobs that may be tempting on the surface.

Looking back over the course of my job searches in 2010 and 2012, I spent hours upon hours applying for jobs that weren't in line with the target position I was seeking, and in hindsight these were job opportunities I should have simply let fall by the wayside. The temptation to disregard peripheral positions is a difficult feeling to overcome, and takes discipline. The bottom line is before you apply to a job, sleep on it for a night. Ask yourself if the position is in line with the role you originally set out to find. Ask yourself if you see a long term career with the company. Ask yourself if you see a long term career in the industry. Ask yourself if you could envision staying in that role for at least two years. If the answer to any of these questions is "no", I would resist pursuing the job. I know that can be a tough pill to swallow at times, but I can assure you, it's a far worse feeling finding yourself in the midst of a job interview for a job you're not really interested in.

So what is a desperate job seeker to do? I suggest shaking things up a bit. It may be time to consider going down an alternate path rather than pursuing the path you originally set out on. Needless to say, the purpose of deviating from your existing game plan is to generate more opportunities. However, you must realize that in order to generate more opportunities you may also need to make sacrifices. In other words, there are no free lunches here. So what do you have to offer in return for more opportunities? The first is location. Now during my 2012 job search I was living in Washington, DC, but my focus was on returning to Boston. When I decided I needed to expand my geographic search I did so in areas that made logical sense, I started looking in Providence, RI, Stamford, CT, New York City, Washington, DC, Baltimore, MD, and Northern VA. These areas were either in my own backyard, or in close proximity to my primary target. Each of those cities I just mentioned had a strategic significance, and more importantly a means of eventually getting back to Boston. When considering, and/or selecting, alternate locations consider the following –

1. What locations make the most sense logistically? Remember, moving 300 miles is far easier than moving 3,000 miles. Also consider how far and how often you will need to travel to visit family and friends.

2. If your end goal is to make it to a specific state or city, then which alternate locations will best assist you in attaining that goal? For instance, you should be considering the strength of your network in alternative locations. Personally, I knew my networking base in New York City would be significantly stronger than say Miami, Florida. Furthermore, a networking base in New York would be far more likely to have connections in Boston than say a network base on the West Coast or Midwest.
3. Realize that if you land a job in some alternate location other than your target region, you will very likely be going through another job search to get to your primary destination.

The second strategy you may undertake to unearth new opportunities, if expanding your geographic region is not an option, is to broaden the scope of your job search. If you've been pursuing a very specific job for an extended period and have made little progress in securing that job then perhaps it's time to loosen the reins, and look for logical opportunities that are closely related to your intended target. Logical opportunities, otherwise known as "transitory roles", ensure that you will continue to, or begin to, develop the appropriate skill set necessary to make you a viable candidate for your ideal job. Perhaps you already know what these transitory roles are, maybe you don't, but either way, do your homework. If you're not sure whether or not a transitory job will help you secure your "ideal job", or if you're not even sure which transitory jobs you should be looking at, then I suggest you raise the topic during your networking calls. This is an easy and thoughtful topic to discuss. Your networking counterpart should have a relatively easy time making suggestions at what type of transitory roles you may want to consider.

This now leads me to the second part of our discussion on desperate times, which is what not to do when you've become desperate. I advise against simultaneously expanding the geographic range of your search, while also exploring transitory positions. Choose one path or the other. You're giving up a lot by pursuing either alternative, and by pursuing both at the same time, you'd be selling yourself short.

Another trap you want to avoid when desperation sets in is over-applying to jobs at a single company. Let's say for example you would love to work for Company X. In fact, you're so passionate about Company X that you're indifferent about the type of role with the company, you just want in. I see this happen all the time. Job candidates take the approach that they'll "get their foot in the door" and work their way up the ladder. Under such a strategy a candidate would apply to numerous jobs at Company X, without regard to division of the company or career level, hoping to get a call back for at least one. Bad idea, my friends. Companies these days track who is applying for what jobs, and how many times a candidate has submitted their resume. A candidate who is applying to a multitude of unrelated positions at a given company does not come across as motivated, but rather comes across as a candidate that is confused about the direction of their career. That is a candidate that most companies are not interested in. You need to be selective and focused in your pursuit of job opportunities, and be mindful of the number of times you submit your resume to a given company.

Chapter 6: Recruiters and search firms

At some point during your job search you're likely to cross-paths with a recruiter, it's almost inevitable. I will tell you up-front that I've rarely had success with recruiters over the years. However, that is not to say recruiters aren't helpful, they certainly can be, and many job seekers owe their success in obtaining employment, either directly or indirectly, to a recruiter. Before engaging a recruiter it's important for you to understand how recruiters work, and what they can and cannot do for you as a job seeker. Rookie job seekers often have overly optimistic expectations of recruiters, and when a recruiter fails to meet those expectations, there is a sense of disappointment.

Having spoke with many recruiters over the years I've certainly observed some trends. I'd like to share my observations with you which will hopefully allow you to establish more realistic expectations for when you commence working with a recruiter.

Let's assume for a minute you decide you want to make a major career change from marketing to finance or, perhaps the move is more subtle, say a change of roles within the finance industry (either situation is applicable). A friend or colleague refers you to a recruiter that they think can be of assistance to your job search. You decide to reach out to that recruiter, unaware of the specific searches the recruiter is actively working, but optimistic the recruiter will be able to help you secure a job in your particular industry of choice. Although the recruiter is likely to be receptive to your call because of the mutual connection, you will likely get a statement at the end of the call that goes something like this, "(insert your name here) you have a great resume, and come across as a great candidate. I don't have any positions at this moment that match your interests or skill set, but I'll reach out to you if I'm working on anything that appears to be a good fit". Now after you have this call (and you most certainly will at some point) please don't hang up the phone and expect that the recruiter is going to call you back in a week and hand you your ideal job with a bow on top. The chances of that happening are quite slim. Let me explain why.

During my last job search in 2012, I spoke with a handful of recruiters. One recruiter in particular was very up front with me and what he said was quite enlightening. He told me (and I'm paraphrasing a bit) that I had a great resume, but it was not his job to fit a round peg through a square hole. I don't know why I had never thought of that before, perhaps it was my naivety, but what he said to me that day made total sense. Recruiters, particularly those on a retained search (i.e. recruiters paid an ongoing fee by the hiring company to search for a candidate), are paid to find candidates that have work experience that exactly matches a client's requirements. Recruiters are not paid to find a candidate that has excellent work experience in a peripheral job function and then try to sell that candidate to the client. An example will help illustrate the point.

Suppose you owned a small French bistro and decided rather than spend time searching for employees you will hire a recruiter to find you the best employees. Now if you asked the recruiter to hire you a pastry chef but the recruiter kept bringing you resumes of grill cooks, you probably wouldn't continue to use that recruiter. Yes, the grill cook works in the kitchen, likely has some excellent cooking skills, and maybe even went to an elite culinary school, but he's not the right person for baking pastries. Even if the grill cook has the fundamental skills necessary to learn the pastry trade, as an owner of a new bistro, you aren't interested in training the grill cook in the art of pastry making. You would likely want a chef that can step right in and start baking croissants. Hopefully you understand my point here. The bottom line is that recruiters are not paid to sell the candidate to the client. The candidate's work experience should largely sell itself.

This now begs the question, what is a recruiter's ideal candidate? I will answer this question in two ways, from my perspective, which is based on my interactions with numerous recruiters over the years, and straight from the source.

Based on my experience a recruiter will give you their utmost attention if you are already working in a role that matches the recruiter's assigned search. Remember the recruiter is trying to seek out the candidate whose makeup is most closely aligned with the required qualifications of the role. The least complicated and most efficient method to complete this task would be to find a candidate that is already in that position within another company. However if you come across a role posted by a recruiter, and in your heart of hearts you know you are qualified for that role, even though you're not already performing that exact job function, who am I to tell you not to call the recruiter? There is always a chance you may be able to convince the recruiter to submit your resume to the company, just don't assume it's a sure bet.

Now suppose once again you are referred to a recruiter (which happens frequently as everyone seems to know a great recruiter!), but come to find out that recruiter is not working on any searches that you're interested in, or has searches that you are interested in, but not qualified for. Although you're likely to get the "we'll be in touch when something comes across my desk that matches your skill set" comment, there may still be some value in having an ongoing dialogue with that recruiter, particularly a seasoned recruiter. Let me explain why. On numerous occasions my conversation with a recruiter would end with the recruiter saying, "if you come across a position you're interested in, please let me know because I have a lot of contacts with financial firms in Boston, and perhaps I can make an introduction for you." Now if presented with an offer like this, don't wait for a position to surface at the company of your choice before taking the recruiter up on his offer. Take that offer today and start leveraging the recruiter's network. I have found recruiters that I am referred to are particularly accommodating to such requests, so give it a shot.

Recruiter Q&A

Job seekers may find it challenging to develop an honest transparent relationship with recruiters. This is a common hurdle in the job seeking process. After all, recruiters are in the business of sales. But who are they selling to, and who exactly do they work for? These, along with a number of other fundamental questions, are important to have answered so that when working with a recruiter you know exactly where you stand in their world. However, job seekers are reluctant to ask these questions because they feel awkward in doing so, or there is the perception the recruiter may be offended. Moreover, even if a job seeker were to build up the courage to ask those thorny questions, they are likely to receive some sugar coated response from a recruiter who is careful not to tarnish their reputation, the reputation of the their firm, or the reputation of recruiters in general. Well ponder these questions no more my friends. The time has finally come for you to receive unfiltered answers to all of those questions we have longed to ask.

To help me with this section of the book I have entrusted the expertise of a recruiter who I knew would provide genuine answers to my questions. The recruiter assisting me has been working in the industry for 30 years and has been President of a global retained search firm, specializing in the technology sector, since 1987. At the request of the recruiter, I will be keeping her name and the name of her firm anonymous.

Before we dive into the Q&A there are a couple of key terms that will be used throughout the discussion that you should be aware of. The first is "retained search firm". A retained search firm is paid an ongoing fee (the "retainer") by the client to find a specific candidate. So unlike a "contingent search firm" that is only paid once the search is completed, a retained search firm is paid both during the search (think of this as salary), and at the completion of the search (think of this as commission).

Now let's dive into Q&A with the recruiter, shall we?

Author: Generally speaking, are recruiters in the business of assisting job seekers find jobs or in the business of assisting clients (i.e. companies) fill open positions?

Recruiter: In general, all recruiters, whether retained or contingency, are ultimately focused on assisting their client (the employer) in filling an open position. In the process of filling the job, regardless of the business model and methodologies employed by the recruiter, results in a placement fee – the end goal for any recruiter. Simply put, recruiters are in the business of making placements- that's how they earn their living in this profession.

As a side note, the job seekers should keep in mind that not all recruiters will provide the same level of quality, focus and ethics during the placement process. I would recommend that any job seeker be selective in choosing the right recruiter(s) to work with - to understand the differences in their business model, methodologies, and style in order to determine who they want to work with and engage in a relationship.

Authors take: Ultimately the recruiter is serving the interests of two parties, the company that hired them and themselves. Unfortunately, in terms of whose interests are prioritized during the recruitment process, the job seeker is likely to find themselves at the bottom of the list. Is it that far fetched to think a recruiter could push a candidate on a company even though the candidate is not qualified, or perhaps the recruiter pushes a qualified candidate on a company even though the job may not be in the long term interest of the candidate? I'm certainly not implying that is how recruiters operate, but I imagine there are some bad apples out there, so keep an eye out for your own interests.

Author: Help me understand when a job seeker should work with a contingency search firm versus a retained search firm, and vice-versa.

Recruiter: Contingency firms (CF) are always working on a large number of job openings for multiple clients in diverse industries or markets. As such, the main advantage to a job seeker working with a CF is the exposure to a broader range of clients and potential job opportunities within diverse markets.

Retained firms (RF), on the other hand, tend to be very specialized in the industries and markets they service. The larger RFs are organized into practices for each area of specialization with recruiters assigned to a specific practice. In addition to being specialized and very knowledgeable in the markets they serve, their relationships with the clients are typically longstanding and exclusive. As such, RFs tend to work with a select/limited number of clients and have fewer job opportunities with very stringent requirements. If the job seeker can connect with a RF that specializes in their field, and are qualified for a specific search, they will reap the benefit of more behind the scenes coaching, and will 'compete' with a smaller field of candidates (4-6) for the job.

Active job seekers should work with both CFs and RFs. And in all cases, the job seeker should be selective and 'interview' the recruiters they are considering working with, to understand their business model/process and their relationship with the employer.

Author's take: There are puts and takes to working with retained search firms or contingency search firms. Retained search firms have closer relationships with the hiring company, while on the other hand, contingency search firms have access to a deeper pool of hiring companies.

Author: Under what circumstances will a job seeker secure a recruiter's undivided attention?

Recruiter: A candidate who has clearly defined and realistic career goals as well as realistic compensation requirements and is a strong communicator will establish themselves as a viable candidate in the eyes of the recruiter. In addition, a candidate who responds in a timely fashion to requests for resume revisions, debrief calls after interviews etc., and strong follow-up skills with both the recruiter and client is favorably looked upon. Communication is the real key to a strong relationship with a recruiter. Candidates who do not return calls, go M.I.A. during the interview process, do not provide info requested in a timely fashion and are not forth coming with their job search status with other recruiters/companies become a real concern and detriment to a successful working relationship.

Author's take: Professionalism and a sense of realism go a long way with recruiters. However, the most important aspect of capturing a recruiter's attention is the viability of your candidacy "in the eyes of the recruiter."

Author: There have been a number of instances over the years where friends or business associates have recommended I reach out to a recruiter that they have worked with in the past. In such an instance is a job seeker making poor use of their time by blindly reaching out to a recruiter that may not be actively in the midst of a search that is well suited for the candidate (i.e. "cold-calling" the recruiter)?

Recruiter: In general, recruiters are not receptive to cold calls, especially retained search firms. Because the recruiter is always focused on developing candidates who meet the criteria of the search they are working, the job seeker can make better use of their time by either sending the recruiter an email inquiry (with their resume) referencing the referral or asking the friend/colleague to make an inquiry on their behalf. Either approach is a more efficient way to find out if their background is of interest to the recruiter for either a current search or future search assignments. If the recruiter is interested, they will pick up the phone and call the job seeker. If neither is the case, the jobseeker can always inquire about a referral to a more appropriate recruiter. Most recruiters are happy to refer job seekers on to colleagues.

Author's take: It is appropriate to engage recruiters under two circumstances. The first of course is obvious, if you are well suited for a search the recruiter is actively working. The second is if you are referred to the recruiter by an associate, family, friend, or colleague. Cold calling a recruiter to introduce yourself seems to be a poor use of time, particularly if the recruiter does not focus on your segment of the market.

Author: When you get off the phone with a job seeker who is not qualified for any particular search that you are working, what do you do with that individual's profile?

Recruiter: If the candidate is professional, a strong communicator and has an attractive skill set which could be appropriate for future search work, we automatically enter that 'future' candidate into our data base along with their resume and cover letter (if it contains relevant info) and details on their job search parameters. This is beneficial to the job seeker because most recruiters defer to their existing database first when launching a search before 'reinventing the wheel' and starting the cold recruiting process. The latter is very time consuming and is likely to be a hindrance in executing a 'rapid cycle time', something that clients are always looking for from the engaged recruiter. Further, the cold recruiting process entails a higher level of risk for the recruiter. The typical search process is first to do a detailed query on the recruiter's existing database. Our firm always makes a point of exhausting contacts within the existing database before we begin cold recruiting. All recruiters, retained and contingency alike, prefer to make a 'quick hit' to keep their client 'happy and engaged'.

Author's take: You should be happy to hear that even if you're not a match for a recruiter's existing search, but maintain a fundamental skill set the recruiter finds attractive, your resume will not fall into a black hole and, in fact, may be dialed back up for future searches.

Author: I imagine recruiters who have been in the industry for some time have amassed a deep network of contacts. If a well qualified job seeker reaches out to you, would you be willing to introduce that candidate to people within your network that may be able to further assist the individual in their search.

Recruiter: If a candidate is well qualified, but their background is not in my area of expertise, I am willing to make an introduction to other recruiters in my network that may be better suited to assist the candidate (based on areas of specialization).

Moreover, if the candidate is seeking employment with company X, but I am not working on a search at the moment with company X, but have in the past, there are other ways I can assist. If I truly believe that the job seeker is of the caliber that my client typically looks for, and/or has the basic 'tool box' that my client would typically look for, and/or is working for a direct competitor of my client, I would definitely refer their resume to the appropriate manager at company X. In fact, I often will be proactive on this front: when I am approached by a job seeker who is actively looking, but may not fit into a particular search I am actively working, I will suggest that the job seeker send me a list of companies they are interested in pursuing as part of their job search and explain that if I have an existing relationship with a hiring manager at any of these companies, that I will be happy to approach the hiring manager to see if there may be a need in their organization for the job seeker. This becomes a rolling process, as the job seeker identifies other companies, he/she will send the names to me. If I do not have a relationship with the company of interest, I will be honest with the candidate so that they can approach the company through their own means.

Author's take: Recruiters may be more helpful to your job search than you initially thought. Use recruiters for their vast network, not just a means to submit a resume.

Author: How can a job seeker maximize their time when it comes to interacting with a recruiter, so no one's time is wasted?

Recruiter: The candidate should be honest about their search parameters. I have had candidates who state one thing during the front end of the process and then at the end of the process, especially at the offer stage, withdraw their candidacy due to a 'change' in their expectations (e.g., salary, distance they are willing to commute, or willingness to actually move). So often candidates enter into the interview process with a clear understanding of compensation and relocation requirements, but somehow hope that it will change if they become the candidate of choice. This becomes a huge waste of everyone's time. Candidates also need to be honest about the status of their job search. If they are expecting an offer from another company they need to be forthcoming about the timeframe and availability to interview vs keeping it a 'secret' for fear that the recruiter will not present their credentials or schedule an interview. This is not fair to the recruiter or the client.

Author's take: Be honest and transparent with recruiters, otherwise you may destroy a potential valuable relationship.

Author: A common response I would receive from a recruiter following an initial inquiry would be, "I'm not working on anything that fits your skill set at the moment, but please reach back out to me every 4-6 weeks and let me know your status." Is this really just a polite way of the recruiter saying, "I can't help you" or is the recruiter genuinely interested in staying in touch with the candidate?

Recruiter: If the recruiter suggests follow-up communication, they are typically being genuine. I do not make this suggestion to everyone - only those job seekers whom I feel may represent a candidate of interest for future search work and I don't want to lose track of them.

Author's take: This is positive news. When a recruiter says follow-up with them they likely mean it, so be diligent and touch base with the recruiter every 6 weeks.

Author: Are there any general rules of thumb as to how a job seeker can select the best recruiter to work with?

Recruiter: It's important to select recruiters who truly understand what you do, and work on searches which require your core competencies and skill sets. Casting a huge net is not necessarily the route to go. It is better to pick 4-5 recruiters who are working on searches in your 'wheelhouse' and establish a good working relationship with them. If possible, I believe it is more effective for the candidate to try to form solid relationships with *retained searched firms* (rather than *contingency search firms*) who maintain strong and longstanding relationships with their clients. As a job seeker, you don't want to be one of ten candidates that the recruiter 'throws' in to the interview process in hopes of making a placement, which I see happen all too frequently when candidates work with contingency firms. For the contingency firms the process becomes all about the placement, versus forming a relationship with the candidate. Job seekers need to 'interview' the recruiter as much as they are interviewing you! Don't be afraid to ask questions regarding their relationship with the hiring manager, how long they have been working on the search, etc.

Author's take: *When possible work with a small group of specialized retained search firms. Keep in mind that certain recruiters are all about making the sale, meaning your interests may take a backseat.*

Author: Based on your answer to my last question, it appears that a contingency recruiter is more likely to submit multiple resumes to the hiring manager than a retained search recruiter. This could potentially increase the competitiveness of the candidate pool. Am I correct in my assessment?

Recruiter: Unfortunately, the vast majority of contingency firms (CF) train their recruiters to the 'numbers game' approach to this business. CFs are focused on making placements with most placing quotas on their recruiters as with any other sales organization. So unbeknownst to the job seeker, they typically become one of 5, 10 or more candidates that are being submitted for the same job. Many CFs will actually have business development teams who bring in the job orders and then put them out to the 'bull pen'. Therefore, one or more of the recruiters at the CF can work the job order – so not only is the job seeker one of many for the recruiter they are working with, but also competing against other candidates being submitted by other recruiters in the same agency. Again, the job seeker needs to ask questions and really filter out the CFs so they know exactly what to expect.

Author's take: Remember to ask questions not just about the job, but how the search firm operates.

Author: I suspect it reflects poorly though when a CF submits a mass of resumes to a client for a particular role. From my perspective undertaking such a strategy reflects that little due diligence was done by the recruiter, they are simply throwing a bunch of resumes against the wall and hoping one sticks.

Recruiter: It's actually quite the opposite of your conclusion. Many clients will demand that they receive a flow of resumes from the CF. On the other hand a retained search firm or exclusive CFs have different approaches to the process, starting with the relationship they form with candidate, as well as the expectations of the client. For example, my clients do not expect me to present more than 3-5 candidates for any one search. As a retained search firm the job criteria that our clients require is so specific that it is very difficult to find more than a few candidates that have the appropriate experience, fall in to the designated salary range, and are willing to relocate (quite often our searches are nationwide). This is a far different model than the contingency firms whose focus is on local markets, and volume over quality.

Prior to starting my own firm, I worked under both business models. When it came time to launch my own business, I decided to go with the retained search approach to recruiting.

Author's take: *Once again, know who you are working with and the approach the recruiter's firm is taking to fill the position.*

In this chapter I discussed how you can maximize the utility of your relationship with corporate recruiters. Further, you learned about the different types of recruiters you may encounter, and how each of them approaches the recruiting process. To sum up my thoughts in one sentence - recruiters do hold some moderate value in a well-rounded job search. However, depending on the job you're seeking, your level of experience, and timing, that level of value add can differ substantially from candidate to candidate.

Before we leave this section there is one concept I want to reinforce when it comes to recruiters. Do not assume for a second that once you connect with a recruiter that the recruiter will be scouring the job market day and night looking to place you in your next role That would be wishful thinking, and is simply unrealistic.

Part II. Interviews and offers

Chapter 7: Interview preparation techniques

Now we will move on to part two of the book which covers interviewing preparation, the act of interviewing, job offers, and what to expect post offer.

If you've already secured an interview then let me be the first to congratulate you. Your hard work has paid off, and you're half way to a new job. Having secured an interview you should be confident that management, or at least someone in the human resources (HR) department, believes you are qualified to perform the basics of the job. Now you just need to prove them correct. Your initial interview will either be with HR over the phone, or perhaps, although less likely, a direct face-to-face meeting with the hiring manager. Regardless of who the interview is with, you must take it seriously. My goal in this section of the book is to break down the interview preparation process into clearly defined categories. Over the years I have developed a method of interview preparation that I have used time and time again, and it has never failed me, ever. I go into every interview with confidence knowing that I will be presenting myself in the best manner possible.

Let's take a step back and think about interviewing from a high level. You've already secured the interview, meaning someone has cross referenced your resume to the qualifications of the job and that person deemed your experience to be reasonably adequate for the position. In this job market, with so many qualified candidates on the street, there is no reason for a company to bring in mediocre candidates to interview. Therefore, assume you're not having the interview simply because the hiring manager needs more information to determine if you can effectively execute the tasks of the job. What the interviewer is really interested in are those traits that a resume simply can't convey (e.g., personality, communications skills, ability to listen, confidence, etc.) The interview pool will likely be between 3-6 other candidates, sometimes more or sometimes less depending on the unemployment rate (there is a positive correlation between the unemployment rate and the candidate pool).

The reality is that you are more likely to leave a lasting impression on the interviewer with a poor performance than a magnificent performance. Often times the candidate selection comes down to a process of elimination, rather than a single individual standing out among the group. Job interviewers may choose to select a candidate based on a process of elimination because selecting the 'best of the bunch' is often too difficult. Interviewers are looking for someone that presents themselves in a professional manner, is confident (not cocky!), has a personality that would mesh well with the rest of the team, is balanced emotionally, and can convey, in a clear and concise manner, how they will add value to the organization. Remember, the interviewer already assumes you can adequately perform the basics of the job based on their assessment of your resume. Unfortunately your ability to perform the basics of the job are unlikely to be enough to land you the job.

If you're like most candidates who have an interview scheduled, your initial concern is what the interviewer may ask of you. There is only one way to get over your fears, and that is to prepare for anything the interviewer may ask. That task may seem daunting, but it's not all that bad when you break it down into smaller tasks. In my experience there are twenty questions that you should always be prepared to answer. In fact, it's almost inevitable that many of these questions will surface at some point in your job interview. You may be wondering about the other million questions the interviewer could potentially ask of you. Well have no fear, if you are able to answer these 20 questions, you can answer almost any question the interviewer will ask, and I will show you how.

These questions appear in no particular order of significance.

1. Walk me through your resume.
2. Tell me about your organization and time management skills.
3. What are your professional strengths and weaknesses?
4. Why are you leaving your current job?
5. What specifically attracts you to this job and/or company?
6. Why do you want this job?
7. What do you like about your current job?
8. Tell me about (job X or company X) from your resume?
9. Where do you see yourself in (X) years?
10. Tell me about your accomplishments.
11. Tell me about a challenge you've encountered in the workforce, and how you overcame it.
12. How would your coworkers describe you?
13. Describe a project you've worked on.
14. Tell me about these (fill in the blank: training courses or college courses or graduate school courses) you took.
15. Do you prefer working in a large group or small group?
16. What are your salary expectations?
17. Do you have any questions for me?
18. Describe yourself in X number of words or one sentence (pops up occasionally)
19. Tell me about yourself. (This question will be asked in a non-work related context. The interviewer wants to hear about your personal

interests, outside of the office. Be ready for this question, it will show up when you least expect it.)
20. Do you have any final thoughts you'd like to share? (this isn't a question you're likely to encounter however you must be ready to make your final sales pitch to the hiring manager)

It's important to realize that the interviewer may not ask these questions exactly as they appear above, but rather may ask some variation of these questions. However, your answer can still be applied quite effectively to those alternative questions. Let's go through a couple of examples. Suppose the interviewer states the following during an interview, "Walter, I see from your resume that you had an opportunity to do some engineering work on the Hoover Dam. That's excellent experience." Now you can see that the interviewer did not specifically ask a question, the interviewer simply made a statement. However if I was in Walter's seat I would have interpreted the interviewer's statement as, "Walter, tell me about the Hoover Dam project you worked on?". Of course Walter should have a prepared answer for this question (it's #13 on the list) and should immediately jump in and start describing the Hoover Dam project because it's quite obvious the interviewer wants to hear about it. The situation I just described is a perfect lead in to a favorite rule of mine which is the more you talk, the less the interviewer talks, and hence the fewer questions you are asked. Please do not interpret this rule as a license to ramble, it certainly is not. The rule simply means that if an offer to speak presents itself, than take the offer. Further, if your answer is well constructed, like a good story, then your interviewer will remained captivated.

Let's look at another example. Suppose the interviewer states, "Tommy, in the job you're interviewing for it's likely you will encounter problems that arise unexpectedly, and those problems will typically be time sensitive. Are you able to quickly analyze and address challenging situations that may arise?" Now Tommy didn't prepare for this exact question, however he has prepared for a couple of other questions that are very much applicable here. For instance, if I were Tommy, I would answer the interviewer's question by providing my prepared answer for "tell me about a challenge you've encountered in the workforce, and how you dealt with it?" (#11 on my list). Hopefully you are getting the point that even if you are not asked an identical question from the list, you are still VERY capable of answering nearly any question that will be asked of you.

Let's look at one more example for good measure. Suppose the interviewer states, "Jennifer, what makes you qualified for this job?" You should be catching on by now. How would you respond to this question using one of your prepared answers? This wasn't one of the twenty questions from the list, but we can certainly answer it. If I were Jennifer I would immediately jump into the answer I prepared for "what are your professional strengths?" (#3 on the list) and that would be a perfectly suitable answer to the interviewer's question. The challenge in all of this is hearing the question, translating the question into one which you have prepared an answer, and then answering the question. Of course the listening and translation portion must be done in your head in a matter of 3-5 seconds. No one said this was going to be easy, but I promise if you practice, the whole process will become natural.

The interview preparation method I'm about to share with you is one in which I developed over a five year period and have used during four separate job searches in 2007, 2009, 2010, and 2012. This method has proven to be quite effective for me, as I'm sure it will be for you too. Now that I have shared with you the "must know" questions every interviewee should be prepared to answer, the next step is to actually answer each of those questions. Pull up to your computer, pop open the word processor of your choice, and start answering each of the 20 questions. There are no short-cuts here.

When answering each question keep in mind a few general guidelines. The first is to be as specific as possible in your answer. As an example, rather than telling an interviewer that you're "motivated", which will undoubtedly leave the interviewer wondering what in the world makes you think you're motivated, give specific examples which depict your motivation. Maybe your answer details how you requested to take on additional projects at work in order to secure a promotion, or perhaps you could discuss how you went to night school to earn your bachelors degree while working full time and studying for a professional designation on the weekend. Those examples depict motivation without even having to actually say the word "motivated". I can't tell you exactly what to write as only you know you're personal situation. The bottom line is to be creative in your answer, and be specific.

My second general guideline when preparing your answers is that each answer should be no longer than 2.5 minutes when spoken verbally, and can certainly be shorter. Anything longer than a 2.5 minute response and the interviewer may start losing focus, and even worse, they may get bored! Furthermore, conveying an answer in no more than 2.5 minutes verbally will force you to consolidate your thoughts. After you write out each answer, read it out loud. After reading it out loud, ask yourself the following, "have I answered this question using general statements?". Be honest with yourself, shortcuts can only harm you in interviewing. If you are speaking in generalities than go back to the drawing board and be more specific in your answer.

The whole process of writing out twenty well-crafted answers could easily turn into hours of work, which is why I suggest you undertake this task before beginning your job search. An interview could pop-up at any moment, and you don't want to be rushed going through your interview preparation. Complete this exercise early and you will save yourself some sleepless nights.

My third general guideline is do not try to provide some overly complex philosophical response to an interview question. No matter how well delivered, you do not want your response to be so complex that the interviewer is unable to absorb its substance. You should be driving towards logical, concise, and easy to understand answers.

Now once you have finally answered each question to your satisfaction, the next step is to memorize each answer. Now don't have a panic attack, this isn't as hard as it may be seem. Just think, actors memorize hours of script for every movie role. You'll be shocked at how quickly you can recite each answer, almost word for word, after reading it a few times. Think of it like this, everyone has a story that they've told time and time again. Well the answers to interview questions often take the form of a story, making it that much easier to recite them from memory. For instance, when the interviewer asks you to walk them through your resume, there is no doubt your answer should unfold like a story, with a beginning, middle, and end. You'll be discussing what brought you to a given job (the beginning), what you learned on the job (the middle), and why you left that job (the end). Remember a good story will always keep an audience captivated.

Ideally you would like to memorize every answer word for word, but the reality is, that is unlikely to happen, particularly with 20 questions. The 30 thousand foot goal of the memorization exercise is to verbally convey each answer in a concise and fluid manner. You should be able to recite each answer without long pauses, and without the use of "umm", "ahh", or "you know" in between sentences. I imagine you didn't write "um" or "you know" while scripting your answers, so those filler phrases shouldn't surface during your interview.

Memorizing answers to interview questions is a two part exercise. The first part involves reciting each answer without looking. Once you have successfully completed this task you're ready for the second part of the memorization exercise which involves reciting answers in a random order. To complete this portion of the exercise you will need a deck of flash cards.

Write each interview question on an individual card. After writing each interview question on a card place all cards face down so the question is not visible. Draw upon the cards in random order and recite each of your prepared answers out loud. This step is instrumental and will give you the ability to react to questions in random patterns, similar to how questions will be presented to you during the interview. I recall many nights sitting in my apartment in the days leading up to an interview, turning the flash cards upside down, and spreading them all over the living room floor. Once the 20 flash cards were spread across my floor I would simply dive in, picking one up, flipping it over, reading the question, and immediately reciting the answer. If I recited the answer to my satisfaction, then I would put that flash card aside, and pick up another immediately (questions will be coming at you one after the next in the real interview, so it's important you replicate that environment). If I was unable to recite the answer up to a reasonable standard, then I would put the card back down on the floor in the same pile with the rest of the unanswered questions.

Another step I recommend taking, to complement the flashcard exercise, is recording yourself while reciting your answers. An audio recording is good, while an audio and visual recording is even better. The feedback you receive by watching and hearing yourself on camera is fundamental to your interviewing development. Often the perception of one's voice and body language is quite different than reality, the microphone and camera will bring this to light. Fortunately, most of us have smart phones these days that allow us to record a film at the push of a button. Take advantage of this luxury.

This exercise in its entirety does an excellent of job of mimicking an actual interview, because unlike the document which you used to memorize your answers, interview questions will come at you in an unpredictable pattern. Once you've made it through each card, take the deck of flash cards, throw it on the floor, and start all over again. I would literally do this exercise time and time again. I would also carry my flash cards with me everywhere, constantly reciting answers when I had some extra time. Eventually the exercise will no longer become challenging, however it may become a bit mind numbing. Admittedly, reciting the same answers over and over again can become monotonous. You'll probably come to hate those flash cards, but you need to continue reciting the answers until you get them right. You must stay focused during this exercise, not simply "going through the motions". By staying focused I mean reciting each answer as if you were actually speaking to someone. I would often sit at my kitchen table, or grab an empty conference room at my office, and envision someone sitting across from me as I recited each answer. I promise you, as painful as this may be, it works.

Two of the twenty questions deserves extra attention, so let's discuss these before moving on.

Question number three inquires about the candidate's professional strengths and weaknesses. Be thoughtful in the answer you choose regarding your professional weaknesses because it can be used against you during the decision making process. I recommend stating a weakness that can no way be perceived as putting the team's goals at risk **and** can easily be overcome. For example, stating that your primary weakness is that you are constantly late will surely hurt your candidacy. Employees that are constantly late can be disruptive to the overall flow of work in a group environment. Finally, regardless of the weakness you disclose, always tell the interviewer what actions you have taking to rectify that weakness.

Your response to question number twenty from the list allows you one final opportunity to sell yourself before the interview concludes. As I stated earlier, it's unlikely the interviewer will prompt you for your final thoughts, rather you will need to provide your final thoughts when you believe the timing seems appropriate. In my own experience, I have yet to be in an interview where there was not an opportunity to share my final thoughts with the interviewer. The conclusion to your interview is incredibly important because it presents an opportunity for you to get the last word in, ensuring the meeting ends on a positive tone.

Your conclusion should be brief (stated verbally in less than 1 minute), and should tie together all the reasons why you are the right person for the job. A conclusion may look something like this:

> *"John, in closing I want to reiterate how strongly I feel about this opportunity with ABCD Corp. This is exactly the type of position I'm looking for where I can leverage my experience in retail marketing as well as the knowledge I've acquired through my graduate level studies. This is the type of organization I'm looking for where I can have a long and rewarding career while working alongside some very talented individuals. When I look at the description of this role I can say with every bit of confidence that I have experience in each of the key aspects and responsibilities of the job. And my primary goal if asked to join this company is to perform my role at the highest level, and add meaningful value to this company's marketing division. Thank you for your time and consideration."*

If you nail the conclusion, which I have no doubt you will, the interviewer will leave the room with a positive perception of you as a candidate. Furthermore, you'll leave the interview feeling optimistic, knowing that you closed out the meeting in a confident constructive tone.

Chapter 8: It's your turn to ask some questions

The final aspect of interview preparation, which fortunately is not nearly as time consuming as memorizing 20 answers, is developing questions which you will ask the interviewer(s). Undoubtedly, once the interviewer feels satisfied that they have all their questions answered, the interviewer will proceed to ask you if you have any questions. Having 2-3 questions prepared for each interviewer is reasonable. Construct questions that show you have conducted your due diligence on the job, company, and industry. Most important, ask questions that are of genuine interest to you. I think an example will help:

> **Setting:** Rosco Hawk is interviewing for a position with Ultimate Apparel.
> **Rosco asks a generic interview question:** 'What challenges may I face in this role?"
> **Rosco asks the same question, but takes a different approach:** "The industry is clearly going through a transitory period where the shift from print to digital advertising is being driven by the rapid consumption of goods and services through mobile devices. While corporations' advertising campaigns must stay at the forefront during this transition, management teams also appear keenly focused on minimizing advertising budgets to achieve earnings expectations. How may this environment of budget balancing, while staying at the forefront of advertising, create challenges for me in this role?"

I think you get the point here. The two questions are substantively similar, except the latter is asked with a bit more thought, and places some context around the question.

The floor is yours so use it wisely. When developing questions for your interviewer there are a few other guidelines which I recommend you follow. First, do not try to stump the interviewer with a question. Questions should be thoughtful, but not overly complex. The intent of the question is to garner information, not to display that you have superior intelligence to the person conducting the interview. When in doubt about the quality or complexity of your question, simply place yourself in the shoes of the person conducting the interview. How would you perceive the question if it were directed towards you? Second, unlike the responses to potential interview questions, I rarely memorize the questions I ask the interviewers. You will be bringing a pad of paper to the interview to take notes. Prior to the interview, section off two pages in your notebook for each person you will be meeting with. Within each section, write down 2-3 questions for each individual. Third, don't be afraid to ask the same question to multiple interviewers. Even if your question was answered sufficiently by interviewer number one, you may find interviewer number two offers a totally different answer, or interviewer number two elaborates on the answer more so than interviewer number one.

In summary, the general rules for compiling interview questions are:

1. 2-3 questions per interviewer
2. When developing a question always err on the side of specifics, rather than generalities.
3. Questions should be thoughtful, but easily interpretable. Do not try to "stump" the interviewer.
4. Questions will be pre-written in your notebook. Allocate 2-3 pages for each interviewer. Leave adequate space between each question in your notebook, because you'll be writing down truncated versions of the interviewers' responses.
5. The Q&A session of an interview is not the appropriate time to discuss salary, vacation, or employee benefits. Your questions should be focused on the industry, company, and job specifics. There will be plenty of time later to discuss salary. There is one caveat here. If for some reason you believe there is a meaningful gap between your salary expectations and what the company may be willing to offer, then you may want to raise those concerns with the human resources representative. However, in reality you should be conducting your due diligence on salary prior to applying for the job as to avoid these types of issues.

Chapter 9: The interview

In my opinion, the interview is nothing more than a reflection of your preparation. The cumulative time you spend preparing for an interview is positively correlated to the likelihood of success on the day of reckoning. Could the interview go poorly even though you were diligent in your preparation? The answer, unfortunately, is yes (albeit unlikely). As an example, let me recap an interview I had in 2011. To this day, it was the longest interview I have ever been through, starting at 9:00 am and ending around 6:30 pm. I did very well through 90% of the interview, delivering all my responses, just as I had prepared them. However, by the last interview of the day (starting around 5:30pm) I was physically and mentally exhausted. Moreover, my final interviewer was intent on stumping me. After a very pleasant introduction, he started to dive into some overly complex technical questions. I had no chance of answering his questions correctly, nor could I have ever prepared to answer such questions. In my opinion the interviewer was less interested in if my answer was right or wrong, and more interested in how I would think through the overly complex problems he presented to me. I simply stumbled my way through his questions providing very uninspiring answers, and yes, it got ugly. The moral of the story is that no matter how much you prepare, there may be variables (e.g., an interviewer intent on stumping you) that are simply out of your control.

This begs the obvious question of how to handle such a situation in which the interviewer starts peppering you with questions, or presents problems, that are beyond your means to answer. The best piece of advice I can offer, if you so happen to find yourself in a situation similar to the one I just described, is do not guess simply because you feel compelled to provide an answer. There is a natural inclination among interviewers to not admit what they do not know. Rather interviewees would rather grasp at straws, an often futile exercise. Should you choose to go down that path, the interviewer may ponder, "is this candidate going to lie to me on the job when he encounters a challenging problem for which he cannot formulate an answer, or is he going to ask for assistance when needed?"

The proper procedure to follow when presented with a problem that is beyond your ability to answer correctly is to work through the problem as far as you can, while simultaneously taking the interviewer through your thought process. Once you get to a point where you are unable to provide at least an educated guess with a reasonable degree of confidence, stop. Explain to the interviewer that you would need to further research the topic before providing a satisfactory answer to the their question. Once again, you need to put yourself in the shoes of the interviewer for a minute and think about how you would react to your answer. Honesty is the best policy, even if that means admitting that you've been defeated by an interview question.

The Interviewers

Throughout the interview process, the individuals you will be meeting with will display different personalities. You shouldn't prepare differently knowing that you will engage in dialogue with various personality types, rather knowing who you may encounter the day of the interview is half the battle. Be aware of the following personalities and more importantly, their expectations.

The "Thinker" Interviewer: The Thinker is a cordial individual who does not want to make you feel uncomfortable, but will ask inquisitive questions to ensure you know what you're talking about. You can identify a "Thinker" quickly by the long (often uncomfortably long) pauses they take while pondering the answer to a question. The drawn out pause is not because they don't know the answer, but rather they want to provide you the optimal answer, which may take a bit more time to formulate.

The "I Don't Know What You're Talking About"(IDKWYTA) Interviewer: I find this type of interviewer amusing. You can identify the IDKWYTA interviewer almost immediately, because everything you say the interviewer's puzzled facial expression will appear as if they have no clue what you're talking about. In fact, the interviewer does understand you perfectly, but has developed a horrible habit of making a terribly confused facial expression when listening intently.

The "Stumper" Interviewer: This is the interviewer whose sole intent is to put you in an uncomfortable situation by asking very difficult (even impossible) questions. The best method here is to take a breath or pause to gather your thoughts, and respond thoughtfully as best you can. These interviewers can be difficult to spot because they may come across as friendly at first, and then quickly turn into something quite the opposite.

The "I Don't Have Time for You" Interviewer: You will be able to identify this type of interviewer very quickly. They will ask you a question, and when you are in the middle of giving your response the interviewer will cut you off and say something like "I got it." Now don't take this the wrong way. Maybe the interviewer felt you gave a sufficient answer, and now would like to move on to a new topic. However, this form of interviewing can be challenging because it disrupts the flow of your answers.

The "Overly Friendly" Interviewer: You get the point here. Maybe this interviewer doesn't even care to discuss the job or the company. In fact, the Overly Friendly interviewer will talk about whatever you want to talk about. In this situation, try to stay focused on business, even if the interviewer wants to discuss the upcoming NFL season. Try not to disregard their lighthearted topics, but instead lightly steer the conversation back to business.

The "Passive" Interviewer: This is my favorite type of interviewer as they will let the interviewee control the flow of the meeting. This is a golden opportunity for you to elaborate on your strengths, or whatever topics you think are the most prevalent.

The "All Business" Interviewer: These individuals are highly inquisitive, and avoid any light hearted conversations. However their intent is not to stump you, rather these individuals simply want to get down to business. Because All Business interviewers have inquisitive personalities and a willingness to listen, try to control the conversation when they're not asking questions. Remember the more you talk the less questions they can ask (this is not a pass to ramble, but rather an opportunity to provide a well thought out, informative, and perhaps somewhat longer answer).

Adjusting to the temperament of your interviewer

One must never forget that an interviewer's recommendation as to whether or not you should be hired is based on how well your personality and their personality can work together. Although you may have a radically different personality than your interviewer, there are techniques that can be used to place the interviewer and interviewee on the same plane. As an example, fast talkers tend to make slow talkers feel uncomfortable, and vice versa. If you're a fast talker, and your interviewer is a slow talker, try to bring your pace down a notch. Taking a sip of water between sentences may help you moderate the speed of your responses. Similarly, if you encounter the All Business interviewer, they do not want to discuss the weather, or anything else deemed as "small talk". Stay focused on more substantive topics and you will make the All Business interviewer feel comfortable. You should be taking a mental note of the personality types of the interviewers you meet with. These are the same individuals you will be dealing with on a daily basis if offered the job, and it's important to consider how your personality and their personality will mesh in a working environment.

Time

During the interview you should always be conscious of time. Nearly all interviews these days are structured to take place within a designated time slot. Some companies welcome a flexible interview schedule, meaning if you run over on time with a given interviewer it's not a big deal, the interview will simply carry on longer than originally scheduled. Other companies may follow a strict interview schedule, which has a hard stop at a specific time. Strict interview schedules may create an uncomfortable situation in which an interview abruptly ends at the designated time, potentially leaving you unable to ask pertinent questions. Therefore, always prioritize the questions you intend on asking your interviewer.

As I've said before, your performance on the day of the interview will be 90% correlated to your level of preparedness. An interviewer's performance can quite easily be compared to that of an athlete's. An athlete's performance on game day has little to do with exogenous factors (e.g., what official is working the game, whether the athlete wears this sneaker or that sneaker, or whether the game is day or night) and more to do with preparation (e.g., time in the weight room, watching film, eating healthy, time on the practice field, etc). Sure, game day is always going to be more difficult than any preseason game, but preparation will surely enhance the athlete's performance on the field, just like preparation will surely benefit you on the day of the interview. Interviewing is also a lot like a standardized test. People spend hundreds of hours studying for exams like the SATs, LSATs, GMATs, MREs, etc. But no matter how much people study, or how many practice exams a student takes, the actual exam will always be more difficult. Interviewing is no different. Regardless though, your success on interview day is made during those hours in your living room talking to the imaginary interviewer sitting across from you, just like excelling on a standardized exam is largely attributed to the hours a student spends completing practice exams.

Now that we've established that 90% of your success on interview day is attributed to preparation, it's important we discuss what accounts for the other 10%. Below are what I consider to be the key variables, which fall outside the realm of core interview preparation, that could meaningfully dictate whether or not a candidate moves forward in the interview process.

The "Other 10%" (in no particular order):

1. Display a sense of passion for the job, industry, and company in which you'd be working.
2. Have a positive attitude, and don't be afraid to smile.

3. Be punctual (showing up late to an interview does not set a good tone, and in some cases could prove to be fatal to your candidacy) .
4. Be well groomed (i.e. shaven, showered, trimmed fingernails, no fragrances, fresh breath, etc.).
5. Dress appropriately (i.e. classy-simple business attire; limited makeup for women, business coats are required for men and women; don't be flashy as your attire should not draw attention; no earrings for men; ensure your suit fits properly).
6. Speak like a gentleman (i.e. no foul language, no inappropriate jokes, avoid slang).
7. Deliver your answers with confidence, but do not come across as cocky. (I'm speaking here primarily to freshly minted college graduates. I know you're ambitious and educated, but regardless of all the internships you've had, or classes you've taken, realize that you still have much to learn.) If you're having difficulty grasping the concept of speaking with confidence without coming across as arrogant, think of how the President of the Unites States delivers his State of the Union speech.
8. Maintain good posture during the interview. (i.e. no slouching in your chair; do not aggressively lean in toward the interviewer; do not rest on your elbows; hands should remain out of your pant pockets)
9. If possible, consume water between interviews not during. Drinking water during the interview is not necessarily inappropriate, but increases the chances of you having a coughing fit, water spilling on you or the table, or some other anomaly.
10. No eating (this includes gum).

You may take some of these for granted, but believe me I have witnessed firsthand candidates get passed over for jobs simply because the basic rules of interviewing were not adhered to.

Chapter 10: The interview is over. Now what?

Now that you have completed your first round of interviewing what do you do next? First off, try not to play Monday morning quarterback, something your author is very much culpable of. Post interview I would find myself focusing on every little detail of the interview that did not go as planned. I would stress about the errors I made (real or perceived), and then convince myself I didn't get the job. Perhaps these negative feelings were a defense mechanism of sorts, mentally preparing myself for the rejection of a job or maybe a hint of pessimism. Either way, it's not healthy and I would avoid going down this path of negativity. Do as thy say, not as thy do, as the saying goes. After the interview stay level headed, and move on. Yes, it's time to move on in your job search. What you don't want to do is sit around dwelling, and waiting for the job you just interviewed for to run its course, which could be weeks, or even months! The quicker you get back to your normal job searching activities (i.e. networking calls, sending out introduction letters, cruising the job boards) the better. But, (there is always a but!) before you move on with your job search, you have some housekeeping work to do.

The first task you need to take care of is to write down your thoughts on the interview. More specifically, take note of what went well, and more importantly, make note of what didn't go well. Document which questions you were unprepared to answer as well as questions you thought you could have handled better. I urge you to do this the same day as your interview. You would be amazed at how quickly the small details from the day will get away from you. I can guarantee, if you complete this simple task, you'll never botch the same question twice.

The second task you need to complete following your interview is sending out "thank you" letters (sometimes referred to as "follow-up" letters). A thank you letter, if you are unfamiliar with the concept, is a letter that the interviewee sends to the interviewer thanking them for their time and the invitation to interview for the position. This has become somewhat of a mandatory task in the interview process.

Every interviewee wants to standout from the crowd and it's not uncommon that interviewees use thank you letters as an outlet to try and separate themselves from the rest of the interview pool. However, too much creativity in your efforts to differentiate yourself may make you seem like an odd duck, and no one wants to work with an odd duck. Sending thank you letters to the individuals you met with is certainly required, but at the end of the day, the content within your follow-up letter is unlikely going to determine whether or not you get the job. Take this task for what it is, a standard requirement, so don't try to get too cute with it.

Job candidates tend to ponder how they should construct and deliver their thank you letters, whether it be an email, printed on a word processor sent via snail mail, or hand written sent via snail mail. While the first two options are certainly acceptable, I would dissuade you from sending hand written letters. Ask yourself this, would you write a hand written letter in your day to day job? Unlikely, so why start now. Besides the fact that writing a hand written letter is unconventional in this day and age, you also run the risk of the person receiving the letter not understanding the content due to poor penmanship.

My recommendation is to send both a mailed letter (written on a word processor) and an email. Why do I say this? First off, the mailed letter will set you apart from the crowd, just enough to be noticed. However, the mailed letter has its drawbacks. First off, it requires that the recipient find a place to store the letter (or perhaps the recipient just discards it). Second, it is not easily transferable to others. Emails, although mundane, take care of these two problems quite efficiently. Emails can be easily saved, retrieved, and distributed among the interviewers if need be.

When it comes to the tangible letter, one piece of advice I can offer is that it is unnecessary to print your letter on expensive letterhead. Doing so doesn't get you any additional brownie points these days, and could make you look like an odd duck stuck in the 1980s.

When constructing the email, and for the sake of convenience to the recipient, I recommend attaching a copy of your thank you letter (in .PDF or .doc format) rather than drafting the thank you letter in the body of the email. By attaching the thank you letter it gives the interviewer the option to save the file to their local drive for reference at a later date. Sure, you could have written the thank you letter in the body of the email (rather than attach a file) and the recipient could simply save the email itself, but there is the risk that the email inadvertently gets deleted or archived to an unknown location.

This now raises the question, "what does one write in the body of the email if the thank you letter is an attached file?" My suggestion is as follows:

Dear Mr. McDougal,

For your records, I have attached a .pdf copy of the letter I mailed to you earlier this week.

Regards,

Rosco Hawk

That's it, short and to the point. There is no need to say anymore. Remember the recipient has already read your thank you letter and if they haven't, they will read the attached document.

Along with your resume, and perhaps notes the interviewer has taken during the interview, the thank you letter will serve as a quick reminder of who the interviewee is, and what skill set they bring to the table. The reality is, unfortunately, that two weeks after your interview, the interviewer will hardly remember the specifics of the meeting with you. That may be frustrating to hear, but it's the truth. Interviewers may be meeting with a horde of candidates, plus they have their own work to deal with, and never mind whatever else they are dealing with in their personal life. When that interviewer is called upon to make a final decision, they will rely on any information they can get their hands on to recount details of the interview, and the thank you letter will serve as a good starting point for them. Finally, if for some reason an interviewer wanted to share a thank you letter with a colleague, or someone else on the interview team, having a hard letter in hand makes that task more time consuming than if the interviewer could simply distribute the letter via email.

In summary, emails and tangible letters both have their benefits and drawbacks. Sending both will ensure you are covering your bases on all fronts.

Now let's get into the substance of your letter. Think about if you were the interviewer, what would you want to see in a thank you letter? Interviewers, for starters, want something short which can be digested easily. They'll be reading a lot of these and will get bored if your letter is more than 1 page.

I have two objectives when writing a thank you letter. The first is to share something I learned specifically from that interviewer to whom the letter is addressed. My second objective is to reinforce my strengths, and how those strengths can add value to the firm. Between those two objectives, it's easy to come up with one page of content. However, I would note that if you can accomplish those two objectives in less than a page, then by all means do so.

Writing this letter should be easy and I'll tell you why. For the first objective, simply reference your notes from the interview. As we discussed in earlier chapters, you should be taking short notes, particularly during the portion of the interview when you get to ask the interviewer questions. Simply use your notes from the interview as your guide. In completing the first objective of your thank you letter you're not only letting the interviewer know they shared something insightful with you (remember interviewers like to hear they did well during the interview too), you'll also be indirectly letting the interviewer know you're an exceptional listener. The second objective of the thank you letter (reinforcing your strengths and how those strengths will add value to the firm) should also not be a difficult task because you have already prepared the answer prior to the interview (see question #3 from the 20 must know interview questions discussed earlier). The bottom line is that writing thank you letters should be fairly easy because all the material you need for those letters will be right at your fingertips.

As stated earlier, think of the thank you letter as more of a standard requirement rather than a differentiating exercise. This does not mean you should skimp on the follow up letter. A well constructed thank you letter in itself will certainly help you stand apart from those candidates that also wrote a letter, but put little effort into it. Blocking and tackling goes a long way in the interview process. The following is an example of a well constructed thank you letter:

> *Dirk McDougal*
> *5555 West Creek Blvd.*
> *Boston, MA 11111*

> *Mr. McDougal,*
>> *It was a pleasure meeting you as well as the rest of the marketing team during my interview last week. I found all the conversations to be quite informative. I enjoyed hearing your perspective on the value of content creation and how without it, the means by which it is delivered is immaterial. I was also impressed to hear of the strides you've made in incorporating mobile technologies as a means of delivering advertising at live events. I have a number of ideas that I'd like to share with you on this front that may help reduce costs related to this mode of content delivery.*

I would like to take this opportunity to reiterate my strengths which will allow me to make a measurable impact on the live events division.

- ***Development of national marketing campaigns:*** *With six years of experience in live events marketing, I have piloted numerous successful national marketing campaigns for global sports apparel manufacturers. Each of which have translated into measurable revenue growth for past clients.*
- ***Contract negotiations:*** *In my current role I have been directly involved in structuring contracts, including project pricing, with both stadium owners and apparel manufacturers.*
- ***Strategically work with cross-functional groups:*** *My ability to collaborate with all parties on a project, including artists, attorneys, apparel marketing teams, stadium marketing teams, and bankers, makes me uniquely qualified for this role with Ultimate Apparel.*
- ***Post graduate training:*** *Since earning my Masters degree in Marketing, I have enrolled in continued education courses to stay up to date on the latest marketing technologies and strategies.*

I would take great privilege joining Ultimate Apparel and even more so by making a meaningful contribution to the future success of the company.

Sincerely,

Rosco Hawk

As you can see from the template, Rosco accomplished his two goals of commenting on something of significance he learned during the interview, and reiterating those strengths which will allow him to add value to the company. Your letter may be longer than my example, but remember, no more than one page.

Now you may receive a response to your letter, however it's more likely you will not. If you do happen to receive a response don't try to overanalyze the content of the letter to determine where you stand relative to the rest of the candidate pool. Typically if you do receive a response it will be brief, something along the lines of "Johnny, it was nice meeting you as well.

Good luck in the interview process." Unless the interviewer asks additional questions of you in their response to your thank you letter, there is no need to send another email.

Chapter 11: Round 2 interviews

As the process goes, if the company was impressed with you during the first interview round, you will more likely than not be invited back for a second round of interviews, or perhaps even a third! When you return for the follow up interview you will likely be meeting a different group of interviewers than you saw the first go around, although don't be surprised if the person you will be directly reporting to wants to meet with you again. Preparing for second and third round interviews is no different than preparing for your initial interview. In fact, the whole reason you're back for another round of interviews is because you impressed in the first round. You must have done something right in your preparation, so stick to the original game plan.

When I was a novice interviewer, one aspect of a second round interview that would always give me anxiety, particularly if I knew I would be meeting with an individual for a second time, was providing redundant answers (i.e. responding to questions with the same answers that I gave during the round 1 interview). Repeating answers should not be of concern to you for two reasons. First, one or two weeks are likely to have passed since you last met with the interviewers. The point I'm making is that an interviewer is unlikely to remember your exact responses from the first interview. If in round 2 you supply the same answers you gave in round 1, the interviewer may hear something that sounds familiar to them, but who cares? They liked your answer the first go around, so why should you be hesitant to give that response to the interviewer again? Second, providing the same answers reinforces who you are, and what you stand for.

The hiring company should always provide you a list of the individuals you will be interviewing with. If this list is not provided to you, then you are in the right to request it. In fact, it is quite common these days that the company will provide an interview schedule as a matter of courtesy. Seeing new names on the second round interview schedule should set your mind at ease in regards to providing duplicate answers, but once again, if you see familiar names on the interview schedule, don't let it bother you. Remember, the interviewers liked what they heard the first time, so give it to them again.

Once you complete your second round interviews you will need to once again go through the "thank you letter" exercise. Even if you don't meet with the hiring manager in the second interview (presumably you met the manager in the first round) it is important to send that individual a second follow up letter. Your second letter to the hiring manager is basically a quick summary of what you learned from the other interviewers in round 2 and how X,Y, and Z reinforces your belief that you are the right person for the job. Use your best effort to get all thank you letters and emails sent within 24 hours after the interview.

Part 3: Post-interview

Chapter 12: References

Candidates that are approaching the culmination of the interview process will be asked to provide references. What appears to be a straight forward process on the surface can cause nightmares for job candidates. What tends to cause complications during the reference process is that the candidate is now bringing multiple independent parties into the mix. The candidate can only go so far in controlling the actions and the words of those individuals. So the bottom line is, do not take this process lightly.

> *Before we dive too deep into the topic of references I want to get a pet peeve of mine off my chest. Occasionally I will see a candidate write at the end of their resume, "References available upon request." Writing this statement on your resume is an unnecessary usage of ink. You wouldn't write on your resume, "I will wear a suit to the interview if required". Of course not. The reality is that a request for references has become a staple in the interview process. There is also no need to provide references early in the interview process, unless specifically asked to do so. The company will typically ask you for references very late in the interview process, often at the point where the company is ready to make you an offer, or if it's down to you and another candidate.*

Ideally, the references you choose should be professional in nature, not a friend, not a family member, not a teammate, not a coach, and not a fellow member of an extracurricular activity. When I say "professional reference" I'm speaking of someone you have worked with. That does not simply mean someone who works at the same company as you, rather I'm referring to someone that can speak to your character, your work ethic, your achievements in the workplace, and your ability to successfully execute the job in question. If for some reason (and it would need to be a good reason) you are unable to secure a professional reference, your reference of last resort should be a professor from your graduate or undergraduate studies (and this is only applicable for recent graduates), someone who you served with in the armed forces, or someone you may have volunteered with.

The company you are interviewing with will typically tell you how many references they require, but if not, don't hesitate to ask. Most companies will want 2-3 references. If they ask for two, provide two, not three, not four, and of course, not one. It's a common courtesy to ask your references for permission to pass their contact information on to the company. By asking permission, your reference will appreciate the gesture of you using them as a referral source, and more importantly, your reference will appreciate the forewarning that they will be receiving a call from your potential employer. When asked to provide references, I recommend providing your references' information in a similar format to what you see in Exhibit 3.

Exhibit 3. Reference sheet

Name	Title	Company	Relationship	Phone	Email	Best time to reach by phone
John Turtle	Dir. of Finance	ZZZ Inc.	Mr. Turtle was my manager at ZZZ Inc.	555-888-5555	tj@zzz.com	1pm
Fred Ocean	Dir. of Ops.	Rick's Tires	Current Manager	555-888-5555	focean@ricks.com	Before 9:30am

The individual contacting your references (likely someone from the HR department) is primarily interested in your work ethic, character, and ability to execute in your potential new role. The conversation will typically start with the human resources representative providing your reference an overview of the job you're applying to, followed by questions that will help your employer determine whether or not you will be able to accomplish the tasks of the new role. The HR rep may also express the company's concerns (e.g., personality conflicts, assimilating into a new culture, ability to work autonomously). Therefore, make sure your references not only speak well, but speak intelligently about you.

Coaching your reference

During my last set of interviews I left no stone unturned, and no detail was too small. One of the extra steps you can take in the interview process is coaching your reference. This process is actually not as uncomfortable as it may seem. Follow these few bullet points to guide your reference to a successful phone call with your potential employer.

1. Provide your reference a copy of your current resume. Now as I said earlier, your reference will ideally be someone you have worked with in a professional environment. Therefore your reference will likely have a general idea of what your role entailed when the two of you worked together, but they might not recall the details. If the reference can't recall the details, they may try to fill in the holes on their own, and that is something you don't want them doing. It's your job to fill in the holes for them, and that can be accomplished simply by providing your reference a detailed resume, and of course encouraging them to review the resume. In doing so, it will assist your reference in speaking intelligently about your role when the two of you were colleagues.

2. Give your reference an overview of the company and position for which you're applying. Generally speaking, the more information your reference has the better. Once your reference understands the role you're going after they will logically start to connect the dots between your previous role (when the two of you worked together) and your potential new role. This will naturally allow the reference to develop some speaking points related to your background.

3. Last, and arguably the most important, tell your reference what the company is looking for in a candidate and what strengths of yours need to be emphasized. As an example, if you know that presenting is a critical component of the job, then let your reference know that. Then point your reference to examples on your resume that emphasize your ability to present. You may also consider reminding your reference of a time you presented in a professional setting when the two of you were colleagues. This will give your reference some easy talking points, rather than forcing them to try and dig into the memory bank on the fly.

The reality is that references will always be somewhat of a wild card because at the moment the reference picks up the phone to speak with the company, you are no longer in the driver's seat. References can, and do, make mistakes. Let me share with you an instance in which I became the victim of a reference's mishap. Although I can laugh at this story today, it was anything but funny at the time.

I was nearing the end of an interview process and I was asked by the company to provide three references. The first reference I provided to the company was a former manager of mine, let's call him Arthur. I knew Arthur would be a great reference. He was well spoken, and thought very highly of the work I performed when we were colleagues. I sent Arthur an email explaining the situation. He was quick to respond, indicating he was more than willing to provide a reference. In his response he also provided the telephone number at which he could be contacted (this is a pivotal moment in the story). After asking the other two references for permission to pass their contact information along to the hiring company, I pulled together a template (just like the one in Exhibit 3) of the three references' contact information and sent it off to the company. Within three days, two of the three references had been contacted by the company however, Arthur, the one I was expecting to give the reference that would lockup the deal, had yet to be contacted.

I began to suspect something had gone wrong. After all, the HR representative that I had been dealing with had ensured me she would be contacting all three of the references. Four days had passed and Arthur had still not been contacted. It was a Friday, and I sent Arthur an email at the end of the day asking (for the third day in a row) if he had been contacted by the company. His response, to my demise, was "no." At this point anxiety started to set in, and I was sure the prospect of a job offer was diminishing. I had not heard from the company in over a week, and my last reference had not been contacted. I picked up the phone and called Arthur. I apologized, and said I had no idea why the company was not contacting him. The reason I apologized is that I knew he had been carrying around my resume and some notes which highlighted my qualifications. When I say he had been "carrying around" these items every day, I literally mean he was carrying around this material with him everywhere he went, because he knew he could be contacted at any time.

Now what happened next was entirely by chance. I don't know what prompted me to ask, but I decided to double check the cell phone number he had given to me. I had the reference table I sent to the HR representative right in front of me, and I repeated aloud the telephone number Arthur had given to me. Arthur, to my horror, says, "No, that's not my phone number." I told Arthur that was indeed the telephone number he provided to me. And just so he knew I wasn't fabricating my story, I pulled up the email he had originally sent me five days prior and recited the number again, this time straight from Arthur's email. He said once again, "That is not my number." My anger started to percolate in my voice and I asked, "what number did you give me?". When he responded that he didn't know what number he had given me, my jaw pretty much hit the ground. I sat there shaking my head, pulling my hair, and yelling profanity under my breath. He apologized profusely and gave me the correct phone number. I immediately updated my reference table and sent it back to the company. I explained to the HR representative that my reference had given me the wrong phone number. Thankfully my HR contact wrote back in short order that she spoke with my other two references, they gave positive feedback, and she didn't see a need to speak with the third. However, she did tell me that she had tried contacting Arthur and was unsuccessful. I passed along the message to Arthur that he would not be contacted. He apologized again for the confusion, as he should have. After all, his blunder could have cost me the job.

Nightmare reference stories like the one I just shared with you happen more often that you would think. In fact, my wife has also had the pleasure of a reference going bad. In the final stages of an interview she had appropriately reached out to her reference (let's call him Bob). She asked Bob if she could use him as a reference and sought his permission to submit his contact information to the hiring company. Bob agreed to be a reference, yet when the HR representative from the company reached out to Bob via email to set up a time to speak, Bob replied he was unable to find the time because he was wrapped up with family matters. This left my wife in the precarious position of having to scramble to find a back up reference. What was frustrating about this particular situation, and in similarity to my own situation, is that my wife couldn't have done anything differently. She asked Bob if he would be a reference, and Bob agreed, making absolutely no mention of other obligations that may interfere with him providing a reference.

The point of these stories is to make you aware that no matter how much time you spend picking the perfect references, and coaching those references, certain variables are simply out of your control. That's reality my friends.

Another situation you may encounter is you are asked to provide references however the company never contacts those references. I have a story to share about such an instance, and I hope by sharing the story it will help you from falling victim to a similar situation. I was interviewing with a well known, highly respected, construction company in 2011. The interview was grueling, probably the most grueling interview I have ever gone through. After hours of interviewing I wrapped up my day by meeting with the hiring manager. During that meeting the manager told me that she thought the interviews throughout the day had gone very well. She then asked me to provide her my references as soon as possible. Well, this was a great sign, or so I thought. The following day I reached out to three references, asking for their permission to submit their contact information to the hiring company. Each reference indicated they were willing to help me out. By the end of that day I had e-mailed the references' contact information to the hiring manager. The hiring manager replied and thanked me for providing the information. It was at that point, when all appeared to be going so well, that things took a turn for the worst. The company did not contact a single one of my references and within one week of my interview, I received a formal letter from the company stating I did not get the job. I was seething. Not because I didn't get the job (that was just flat out disappointing), but because the company didn't contact my references. The bottom line is, if any interviewer specifically asks you to provide references, then they should be fully committed to contacting those references once provided.

You may be thinking, "how do I prevent a situation like this from occurring?" The simple answer is to be forthcoming with the company. During a more recent interview process I went through I was asked to provide references to the hiring company. It had been two years since I was burned by the construction company, yet the memory was still fresh in my mind. So when asked to provide the references I simply stated to the HR representative that made the request that I would be more than happy to provide references, but I wanted to ensure that she would in fact be contacting each of them. She assured me that she would, and she did indeed contact every reference I provided to her. After getting burned once, I will always confirm, when asked to provide references, that those references will indeed be contacted. I recommend you do the same. For a company to ask you for references, and not contact them, is simply unprofessional and unacceptable.

Finally, you should never put your references in an uncomfortable situation. So what exactly do I mean when I say, "uncomfortable situation"? An example would be that you lied on your resume, and then ask your reference to go along with the lie. You absolutely cannot do this. If you lied, then you alone must deal with the consequences. While constructing your resume, know that at some point in time, someone that you are reasonably close with professionally is going to have to confirm some, or all, of the content within your resume. Once again, place yourself in the shoes of the reference. If someone were to ask you to lie, exaggerate, or stretch the truth, I imagine you would think less of that person's character. Moreover, if someone were to ask you to lie, and you were to go along with it, then you would be putting your own reputation on the line. If you, or your reference, lose credibility, your careers may be short-lived. Word travels fast in certain industries, and you never know who is talking to whom. Don't state anything on your resume that you are unable to truthfully back up, it's simply not worth putting your reputation on the line.

Chapter 13: The offer

It's the most exciting part of the interview process, it's what you've all been waiting for. Without further adieu, ladies and gentlemen I present to you, The Offer. Now if you're like me, you've been sitting on pins and needles ever since your references were contacted. At this point, there is really nothing left for you to do, but wait for the company to contact you.

Let's get through the bad stuff quickly. If for some reason the company decides to go in another direction, and proceeds with another candidate, don't be surprised if you simply receive an email stating you weren't chosen. No matter how the message is delivered, and no matter how upset or mad you may be, always act in a professional manner. I strongly recommend writing a very brief email to the hiring manager. Here is an example.

> *Dear Mr. Brady,*
>
> *Although I'm disappointed I was not offered the Analyst role, I welcomed the experience meeting you and your colleagues. I encourage you to keep me in mind for future opportunities that may arise in the marketing division.*
>
> *Sincerely,*
> *Rosco Hawk*

That's it, short and sweet. If you are not cordial and professional after getting turned down for a job, it may bar you from future opportunities with that firm. Firms routinely bring candidates back for future interviews after they were initially turned down; I see it happen all the time. Speaking from my own experience, I was invited back to interview with a company almost three years after I had originally interviewed with the firm. If a manger doesn't hire a candidate, but was impressed with the candidate none the less, they may bring that candidate back for a new opening in their group, or they may hear of a colleague hiring, and pass the candidate's resume along for review, likely with a recommendation. The takeaway is, if you don't get the job, stay on the good side of the company, always act professional, and you never know, you may be next in line when that new role opens up.

Now suppose you get the call you've been waiting for, which will likely come from the hiring manager. They will spend a couple of minutes discussing how impressed they were with you during the interview process and how they are excited to make you an offer. That's nice and all, but let's hear the offer! Make sure you place the caller on hold to get a pad of paper because they're likely to throw a lot at you. The company will typically mail you an offer package the same day the offer is presented, but that could take a day or two to arrive, and you'd like to have all the details of the offer down in front of you to review once you get off the phone.

When making an offer, the manager is going to inform you of the base salary, the bonus (if any), relocation package (if applicable), signing bonus (if applicable), retirement benefits, and vacation. There are so many components to an offer, and a manager may neglect, or forget, to provide details beyond the categories I have listed above. The following is important, so read carefully. No matter how thrilled (or disappointed) you are with the offer do not, I repeat do not, accept (or turn down) the offer immediately. Tell the person you are speaking with that you would like a day to consider the offer. No company has the right to tell you they want a decision on the spot. At a minimum, the company should give you the night to sleep on the offer. When my last offer was made to me I was so excited with the offer that I went against my own advice, and accepted the offer on the spot. You know what the hiring manager said to me? "Why don't you take a couple of days to think about it, and call me at the end of the week." There I was caught up in the moment of excitement and the manager essentially denied my acceptance, telling me to take a few days to think about it. She was absolutely right though, I did need a couple of days to let it all sink in. It's a good thing I took those few days, because after scratching the surface of the offer, I had a laundry list of questions that needed to be answered before I was ready to accept it.

This is a good time to dive into a check list of items you should be comfortable with before accepting an offer.

1. Base Pay
   a. Amount and frequency of pay (i.e. weekly, bi-weekly, monthly)
2. Bonus or Commission
   a. Frequency of bonus
   b. How the bonus or commission is determined
   c. Range of bonus (min/max) (e.g., 10-80% of base, flat 10% of base)
3. Vacation time
   a. If the manager says you get two weeks of vacation per year inquire if that vacation accrues over the course of the year or if you will receive two weeks of vacation pro-rated on your first day of employment.

     b.   Inquire how many vacation days you may carry over per year?

     c.   Inquire if you will receive personal days (sometimes referred to as "floating holidays") in addition to your vacation time.

4. Sick time policy (if applicable, not common in the private sector)
5. Family leave
     a.   Inquire what the leave policy is for new parents and whether the leave is paid or unpaid
     b.   If applicable, inquire about time off to care for sick family
6. Expected traveling per month
7. Telecommuting policy
     a.   Working from home has become common practice these days. Some companies even encourage it as it is a cost savings for the firm.
8. Relocation assistance (typically this is only applicable if you must move in order to work for the company)
9. Commuting benefits
     a.   Some companies may offer a subsidy to those employees that take public transportation.
10. Tuition or continued education reimbursement
     a.   If applicable, it's important to inquire about reimbursement for expenditures to be incurred as well as expenditures already incurred. As an example, say in January you registered for the CPA (certified public accountant) exam which takes place in July. You become employed with your new company in May, prior to the test. You may be eligible for reimbursement of exam registration fees because you will have been employed with the company on test day.
11. Eligibility for pay increases
12. Health and dental insurance
     a.   What is the monthly/annual premium split between employee and employer?
     b.   Does the employer offer both a high deductible and low deductible plan?
13. Retirement benefits
     a.   Does the company offer a 401(k) or profit sharing plan? If yes, than what is the company's contribution to that plan? If yes, than what is the vesting period?
14. Employee review process
     a.   Is the employee's performance reviewed annually or semi-annually?
     b.   What is required of the employee during this process?
     c.   How are results of the review used?

15. Start date
    a. Inquire if there is flexibility in the start date. A 2-3 week window between offer acceptance and first day of employment is normal. If you must move from out of state, than expect the company to give you 3-4 weeks before your start date.

Those are the key topics that should be discussed prior to accepting an offer. If the hiring manager (or human resources officer) doesn't cover any of the topics listed above, then you have every right to inquire. You should not think for a moment that asking any of the questions I listed above will impact the offer that's already been presented to you. In fact, it may come across as peculiar to the hiring manager if you don't inquire about the details of the offer.

If all the questions have been answered to your satisfaction, and you are pleased with the package that has been presented to you, than accept the offer. Like every other interaction you have had with the company thus far, I recommend thinking about what you will say when accepting the offer. A well thought out and gracious acceptance will leave you and your new employer departing the call on a happy tone. What follows is an example of what I consider to be an appropriate acceptance of an offer.

> *"Mike, I appreciate you answering all my questions. At this point, after considering the details of the offer for a few days, I'm happy to say that I'd like to accept your offer. Thank you again for giving me this opportunity, and I assure you that you will not be disappointed in your decision."*

Do I accept the offer, or not?

What if you love the job you're pursuing, but the terms of the offer aren't up to your standards? This is an important topic we need to discuss. There have been three times in my professional career where I have gone through the interview process, been offered a job, yet was unsure if I should accept the offer, or not. Let me share a couple of these experiences, so you can learn from my mistakes, and hopefully avoid this truly precarious position.

It was early 2009, the peak of the recession. I had been laid off from my job in January of that year and had been busting my hump for three months trying to gain employment. After networking my way to an interview, and trudging my way through a long and painful interview process, I was presented an offer. However, my enthusiasm for the offer was lacking. An outsider observing this situation may have thought I very well should have been excited. After all, I had only been out of work for three months, in the midst of the worst financial crisis since the Great Depression, and here I was with an offer on the table, which included a 5% pay raise over what I had been making in my last job. But the reality was, I couldn't get excited. The reason was simple.

In 2007 I had decided to switch career paths and go into the field of commercial real estate investment. I had been employed with a real estate investment firm for just under two years before getting laid off. I enjoyed the real estate investment industry, and for three straight months after getting released I job searched with the sole intent of finding a job in that industry. I was trying like hell to get back in, but to no avail. The real estate industry took it on the chin during the Great Financial Recession. If you worked in the industry, you know, everything came to a grinding halt. To cut to the chase, the company I received the offer from was not in the real estate sector, but rather in the energy sector. Surprisingly, the work I would be doing at the energy company was quite similar to the work I had been performing with the real estate investment company, but at the end of the day it was a different industry, and that did not sit well with me. I felt like I would be giving up on the real estate sector if I took the job with the energy company. However, these were tough times, and there was no daylight at the end of the tunnel for the real estate sector in January of 2009. After a lot of internal debating, I accepted the job with the energy company. My decision to accept the job was done out of desperation. I knew the economy was awful. I had been aggressively job searching for three months with little to show for it. Ironically, every person I networked with over a three month period was in fear of losing their own job, never mind hiring. The job with the energy company paid well enough, the company was doing relatively well given the state of the economy, and the job was similar to what I had been doing previously. Therefore, I accepted the offer. You're obviously now wondering how things shook out for me with the energy company.

Fast forward six months - as you may have guessed, I wanted out of my job, but not for the reasons you may suspect. I actually found the energy sector fascinating, even more so than the real estate sector. However I realized quickly I was being grossly underpaid for the work I was performing. The company undercut me on salary when I was in a bad spot in my career, and I had little leverage for negotiating (it was an employers market for sure). I realized I wanted out after a very short time, but the one bright spot in all of this was that I would be more than happy staying in the energy sector.

There are a few lessons we can take away from this example. The first is that you must understand the condition of the job market before jumping into a job search. If the country is in the midst of a recession than there is a chance you will need to make sacrifices, including a change of industry. Mentally preparing yourself for a change of industry at the onset of your job search is far less painful than doing so with a job offer on your plate and 24 hours to make a decision. The second take away from this example is that you should learn to stand up for yourself and demand fair wages for fair work. If an offer is already on the table the worst possible outcome to your request for a higher salary is the company saying "no". It's highly unlikely that the company would rescind your offer simply because you chose to negotiate your starting salary in a professional manner. The final lesson here, and perhaps the most important, is that a change of industry is not always something to dread. I changed industries kicking and screaming, but I'm quite content with where I am in my career and I would not be where I am today had I not changed industries during the recession.

And the story continues….

After leaving the energy company in the summer of 2010, I found another job in the energy sector. It was a great job, and a good time in my life. This new job and employer received a lot of publicity, and after just a year with the firm, unsolicited offers started coming to me! I had four offers in late 2011 and early 2012, and I hadn't even been job searching. That's how it happens sometimes. So in January of 2012, I had been recruited by a company, went through the interview process, and was made an offer. The offer was good, but once again I found myself in a position where I wasn't sure if I wanted to take it. After about a week of internal deliberating, I decided to turn down the offer. There were a number of reasons that led me to my decision. The company that made me the offer was well-established, however the group in which I would be working in was brand new. From my perspective the group was so new, that it hadn't quite found its identity yet, which meant there were too many unknowns. Given that I'm risk averse, the unknown is somewhat bothersome for me. Second, the service this company performed, although within the energy sector, was VERY niche. That meant if I wanted to leave the company at some point, and go elsewhere, I would likely find it difficult to sell myself into other roles. Third, I asked myself if this job would assist me get to where I ultimately wanted to be in my career. The answer was unlikely. Fourth, I thought to myself, "I'm not even job searching and I've had four offers. If I actually start putting in some effort I could likely find something that suits my long term career goals rather than settling for something that happened to fall in my lap." I politely turned the offer down. That was difficult to swallow given the amount of money I was letting slip through my fingertips. Now let's fast forward four years. In retrospect, I have absolutely no regrets about turning down that offer. In fact, turning down that job was one of the top pivotal moves I have made in my career. Once again, it's highly unlikely I would be in the spot I'm in today, had I accepted that job offer.

It's likely you will encounter similar situations at some point in your own career, in which you are presented with a job opportunity, yet the decision to accept or reject the offer is not black and white. Let me lay out some topics that you should be considering which will help you through your decision process.

First and foremost, you need to think about what you want to do with your career and where you want to be three, five, or even ten years from where you are now. Trust me, I know this can be a daunting question to answer, but if you do have an answer, it will make your decision of whether or not to accept an offer that much easier. However, if you have found yourself in this troublesome predicament of uncertainty surrounding an offer, than I will assume that the job in question is not where you ultimately want to be in your career, and perhaps may not even be a suitable transitory role. I define a transitory role as any job that provides you with the skill set, qualifications, and connections that will bring you closer to your ideal job (I'm reluctant to say "dream job" because after all a job is work!). Taking a transitory role is perfectly fine, and most often times necessary, but you have to be able to connect the dots between your transitory positions and where you ultimately want to be in your career. Start by asking yourself if taking another transition role brings you one step closer to securing your ideal job. If you're currently in a transition role ask yourself if that job has already helped you establish the core skill set necessary to attain your ideal job. If it has, than I strongly suggest you stick to your guns and be a bit more patient in your search, rather than moving into another transition role.

Ideally the question of where you want to be at some later stage of your career should be answered before you start your job search, not at the time an offer is made. I know that some of you may try, but are simply having difficulty answering this question. For those of you in this situation consider the following: Is the position you're about to accept something you could see yourself doing over the long term? As fate (or the economy) may have it, you could find yourself stuck in the position you're about to accept for years and years. Is that something you can live with? Be honest with yourself. Next, ask yourself if your new job would be niche? I'll give you an example of a "niche" job." The freedom of information act ("FOIA") allows any U.S. citizen, for a small price, to request any piece of information from the U.S. government. Every agency of the U.S. government has a group that processes all FOIA requests. I consider individuals that are processing FOIA requests to have a niche job simply because the job doesn't exist outside the federal government. I could be wrong, but I envision individuals in a FOIA role having a great deal of difficulty selling themselves into other positions, particularly in the private sector. So the best advice I can offer, is stay away from niche roles, unless you can envision yourself staying in such a role for the foreseeable future.

Another obvious issue that rears its head in the decision making process is salary. Maybe you love a job opportunity, but the salary just isn't right, or is flat out unacceptable. My advice in such a situation is that you should never accept, or turn down, a position simply based on salary. Obviously there are exceptions here. If you have a mortgage and a family that is dependent on you, than a significantly lower salary may not support your current lifestyle, which is not good. However a more realistic example is one which happened to yours truly. In 2010 I was presented with a job offer with the Federal government. The role itself was perfect in the sense that it was an ideal "transition job". However, the salary was well below what I had hoped for. It was a salary though that could support my lifestyle, with some minor sacrifices. I ended up accepting the job irrespective of my displeasure in the salary, and it turned out to be one of the best decisions I ever made in my career. Although I spent the first year with the government working my behind off (yes, there are hard working Federal employees out there!), knowing full well my salary was ~50% below what similar positions in the private sector paid, I was the happiest I had ever been in my career. I loved my job, and the satisfaction I received from my work made the subpar salary essentially a mute issue. Once I got in my role, salary rarely crossed my mind. I had a great job, which I knew would lead me to a better place in my career, and I was happy. Furthermore, I knew that if I continued to work hard in the role, pay increases would come, and they did. I think you know the point I'm driving towards, but to spell it out in plain English, you can be truly happy in your job with a salary that is not ideal. As a guy I networked with once so eloquently told me, "focus on the job itself, the money will eventually come." He was right.

There are people out there (and I know many) that consider money to be the end all be all of a career, and to each their own. But I promise you that you can indeed be satisfied in a role even with a less than ideal salary, assuming once again it is not disruptive to your lifestyle. Let me be clear though, salary is important, and if you're going to make a sacrifice on salary, then that job better be awesome in every other aspect, and if it is, then you'll be alright. I don't think I would have been able to reach this conclusion unless I lived through the scenario myself.

Another question you may be asking yourself in the decision making process is "should I hold out for something better?" Job seekers often struggle with this question, but the reality is that the answer is often easier than one may think. Once the candidate is able to remove certain factors that are less important in the long run (e.g., salary, title), the answer to the question becomes more transparent. As described earlier, I have dealt with this situation personally. For a week in 2012 I wrestled with an offer and the question of whether I should be holding out for a better opportunity. In hindsight, it shouldn't have been a difficult decision for me. But because the salary was lucrative, I let it cloud my judgment, at least temporarily. In the end, I made the right choice. I decided that it would be best to hold out for something better because the position at hand would not have assisted me in attaining my long term career goals.

You may also ask yourself if you should be holding out for something better if you've been engaged in a job search for an extended period of time. Perhaps you're ten months into an aggressive job search and you've had minimal success, apart from one mediocre offer you now have on the table. Take a step back and be realistic with yourself. Why have you not found your ideal job after a ten month search? Is it because the job market is universally terrible due to a recession? Is it because the job market is very competitive in the city you're looking? Are you simply not qualified for the job you are seeking? These are important questions you should be asking yourself. If you are unsure if you are truly qualified for a particular role, there is a very easy way to find out. You can discover the answer through networking, and asking individuals in the field (people directly in the role you seek or a recruiter who knows the role well). If you are truly qualified for the job you are seeking, both from an educational and a professional perspective, then I suggest continued patience in your search, and remain focused on your ideal job. If you're not qualified for the role, and landing that job would be a stretch, you should consider changing your game plan, and begin focusing on transitory roles. Specifically, focus on roles which will help you fill in the holes in your resume, and give you the appropriate experience necessary to secure your ideal job.

Deliberating over whether or not to turn down a job offer can be difficult, I mean really difficult, particularly if you've been engaged in a search for a while. The easiest way to avoid such a situation is to not place yourself in that situation to begin with. Simply stated, don't pursue jobs that you're not really interested in. I can't tell you how often I found myself applying to jobs which weren't truly appealing to me. So why on Earth would I spend all that time customizing my resume, writing cover letters, and even networking with people at the company if I wasn't truly interested in accepting the position if it were offered to me? There are a few reasons. Often I would have feelings of desperation, and the act of applying for a job gave me a sense of progress in my search. Moreover, perhaps there was some small aspect of the job, and/or company which I found attractive.

Finally, I was lured into applying for a job if I considered myself to be a perfect candidate for the position. Now I very well may have been a perfect candidate for the job, and met all the necessary qualifications, but that certainly doesn't mean it was the right position for me.

Be conscious of these traps I have discussed, as it will save you time, effort, and most importantly, it will help you avoid going so far down the interview path that you are placed in the gut wrenching position of having to turn down a job, or accept a job, that is not entirely suitable to your needs. Honesty is the best policy here. Before applying to a job take a step back and examine the big picture. Is the job you're applying to significantly different than the role that you had initially sought out at the beginning of your search? Are you hopping from one transitional job to another? Are you applying for a position for which you are overqualified? Are you applying for a job out of desperation? Are you applying for a job simply to keep yourself busy? If you answered "yes" to any of these questions there is a strong possibility that you may soon find yourself in a position of having to turn down a job that is not entirely right for you.

Before I leave this topic I'm going to say something that will be entirely hypocritical, but at the risk of confusing you I will say it anyway. As you may have noticed I'm all about practicing the art of interviewing and if opportunities arise for you to practice interviewing, you take them, even if you may not be interested in accepting the job if offered. I'm not recommending you should spend time applying to jobs for the sole purpose of getting interview practice, but if an interview falls in your lap for one reason or another (and this happens more often than you would suspect) you may want to consider taking the interview, even if you are not interested in the job, solely to get some interview practice. Any interview prep time you can accumulate will be tremendously beneficial when game time rolls around.

Salary Negotiations

There will likely come a time in your career when you want to negotiate a higher salary with your employer to be. There are a host of reasons why an individual may choose to negotiate salary, but irrespective of the reason, the approach to negotiation is the same.

Before we move forward with negotiating tactics, there are critical questions that need to be answered:
1. What salary is satisfactory to you?
2. What constitutes a fair offer and why?

Employers will take one of three strategies when making you an offer. The first strategy, which is the most common, is the margin based offer. The second strategy an employer may use is the market based offer. The third strategy is the low-ball offer.

Margin based offers have become common practice these days. Under this method the company will inquire what the candidate is currently earning and then make an offer that is some fixed percentage over that salary. If you work with a recruiter, then I can assure you the recruiter will inquire about your current earnings. Candidates often feel an urge to inflate their current salary by some marginal amount (perhaps 5-10%) with the expectation that the company will employ the margin based offer. Although their line of thinking is generally correct, candidates often forget the fact that a hiring company will inquire with past employers, during the background check, what the candidate's salary was on the last day of employment. If the company determines you lied about your prior salary, your potential offer could be put in jeopardy. Fortunately, you can easily avoid this mishap by simply telling the truth. Although one can expect a pay increase under the margin based method, that doesn't necessarily mean the offer is fair.

The "A-type" companies, as I refer to them, tend to employ the market based offer strategy. Most candidates prefer this method because they know that the offer is fair. Under this method the employer will indeed ask you what you are currently making, but it may have very little impact on what you will be offered. For instance, if you're currently making $35K per year, but the position you're applying for at Company X typically pays $70K a year, then that is what the offer will be, irrespective of the fact that it's a 100% increase to your current salary. In reality, Company X will have a salary range, say $70-85K per year. In our example, because the candidates salary is $35K, the offer will likely be to the low side of the range. However, despite the offer coming in at the low side of the range, the market based approach remains far more lucrative for the candidate than the margin based offer.

The final strategy that a company may choose to employ is the low-ball offer. No candidate wants to be on the opposing side of a low-ball offer as it can be a very deflating experience. Lord knows I've been on the opposite end of numerous low-ball offers in my career. A company may take this approach if it's a generally poor market for job seekers or if you are out of work. Under this method the company will inquire what you are currently making, or what you previously made at your last job if you're now unemployed, and then offer you the same or less than your most recent salary. In my opinion this is a demonstration of poor business practice because it leads to high employee churn. Say for instance a desperate unemployed job seeker takes a 10% wage cut to get back to work, only to find out that the work is more grueling than it was at their previous job. That employee is likely to begin seeking new employment where the salary is commensurate for the work performed. Companies that employ a low-ball offer method may win in the short term, but they rarely win in the long run.

Let's tackle our first question, what salary is satisfactory to you? One of the major follies of a job seeker is not giving serious thought to salary requirements at the very early stages of a job search. That's right, the time to start thinking about your salary requirements is now, when your head is clear and not tainted by the negative variables that can come along with job searching (e.g., stress). As a job seeker you should know what you can't accept, what you are willing to accept, and what you want to accept. The absolute worst possible strategy you can pursue is starting to think about your salary requirements after an offer is already placed in front of you. I say this because once an offer has been made, the time given to you to decide whether to accept or reject that offer could be as little as 24 hours, and the chances of you making an irrational decision increase exponentially. Additionally, if you have no preconceived notions on salary, you may let the offer cloud your judgment. Let me give you an example.

> *Ricky Green is pursuing a position as an Analyst with a Telecommunications company in Tulsa, Oklahoma. Ricky sourced the job opportunity through networking and has been going through the company's interview process for the past two months. Ricky is of the opinion that the position is an excellent transitory role, and he couldn't be more thrilled to work for this particular company. Finally, Ricky gets the call he's been waiting for. It's the company calling, wanting to offer him the position. Ricky is overcome with joy, but his joy quickly subsides once he hears what the company is offering as a starting salary. The salary offered is 5% less than Ricky's current salary. Ricky was certain that the job would have paid him more than his current role. Furthermore, Ricky is informed that there is no room for salary negotiation. Ricky has 24 hours to not only determine if the benefits of the position outweigh the lower salary, but also determine if he can even afford to meet his expenses taking a 5% salary cut.*

I do not want to see you in the same stressful situation as Ricky. Fortunately, there is a very easy way to avoid this situation. If Ricky had answered the two key salary questions during the early stages of his job search, his decision to accept or reject the offer would have been far easier, and more importantly he would be making the decision in advance with a clear mind.

Now let's revisit Ricky's situation, but under a slightly different pretense.

> *Prior to commencing his job search Ricky has determined that he will not accept a position if the offer requires taking more than a 5% pay cut. Moreover, Ricky is seeking a 5% raise in his new role. The telecommunications company offers Ricky a salary that is identical to his current salary. Ricky's salary requirements have been satisfied however, he is not thrilled with the offer. In fact, he would like to negotiate.*

Ricky has already determined, early in his job search, that he would ideally like to receive a 5% pay raise when switching employers, but does he actually deserve a 5% pay increase? This now leads us to our second question, what constitutes a fair offer for the job you're seeking? Your first source for finding salary information should be the internet, however if you run out of luck using online resources consider posing the question to a trusted person in your network, but only if you feel comfortable discussing the topic. If Ricky has done his research and feels that a 5% raise is both justified and realistic, then he should most certainly try to negotiate a 5% raise. I would also encourage Ricky to plead his case to the hiring manager why a 5% increase is warranted. More often than not employers will leave some window for negotiating salaries, which is positive news for Ricky.

Salary negotiations are typically done quickly. You will only have one opportunity to make your case for a higher salary, so make sure you do your research first. I cannot give you specific guidance on whether or not to accept a job based on salary X, Y, or Z because every situation is so different. I will say though that you should absolutely not discredit a job solely because it may pay less than your current role. There are many positions out there in which the experienced gained is far more valuable than the salary received.

Chapter 14: Background checks

We are finally approaching the end of our journey. You've been offered the job, your salary has been negotiated, all of your questions have been answered, and now you're ready to accept the offer. So that's it, right? Not quite, there's one more step before you're in the clear…the background check. The *background check* should not be confused with the *reference check*. A reference check is typically done prior to any offer from the company, while a background check is conducted after the offer has been made and accepted. Most job offers will be contingent upon a satisfactory background check. In my experience the hiring company will not be conducting the background check (primarily due to time and resource constraints), but rather will outsource the task to a company that specializes in such work. These companies are otherwise known as *consumer reporting agencies ("CRA")*. Kroll, Sterling Talent Solutions, and First Advantage are all examples of companies that specialize in conducting background checks. A background check will answer the following questions for your new employer:

1. Was the candidate truthful about prior employment? The CRA will be looking to confirm your dates of employment with past employers, prior titles, and your salary at the time you left a prior employer. Typically, specific duties in your prior role are not confirmed in the background check. Verification of duties is typically conducted during the reference check. It is common practice that the CRA will contact up to three of your previous employers, usually the last three places you have worked. Previous employers can't say too much about your employment history because of potential defamation liability. CRAs are aware of this and should not ask anything that is out of bounds.
2. Does the candidate have a criminal record? Under the Fair Credit Reporting Act, CRAs cannot provide employers arrest records beyond 7 years. However, if the salary of the job for which you are applying is above $75,000, then employers are eligible to go deeper into your past.[12]
3. Is the candidate a "bad actor" (i.e. terrorist)? Companies typically avoid hiring terrorists these days.
4. Has the candidate been truthful about the educational degrees listed on his/her resume? The CRA will typically inquire about the dates

---

[12] The Federal Trade Commission. "Fair Credit Reporting Act" <https://www.consumer.ftc.gov/sites/default/files/articles/pdf/pdf-0111-fair-credit-reporting-act.pdf>

the candidate attended college or graduate school and the degree(s) the candidate claims to have received.

5. Has the candidate been truthful about any designations they claim to have been awarded? There are countless professional designations these days (e.g., CPA, CFA, CFP). The CRA will confirm the date in which the designation was awarded.
6. Is the candidate a sex offender?

You can expect that any CRA will be providing your new employer an answer to each of the six questions listed above. Depending on the job at hand, the employer may also request the CRA to provide citizenship status, immigration records, bankruptcy records, tax liens, credit checks, drug tests, driving history, civil suits, and other. It's also worth pointing out that under guidelines issued by the U.S. Equal Employment Opportunity Commission (EEOC) an employer cannot deny an applicant solely because of an arrest record, as that may create a violation of Title VII of the Civil Rights Act of 1964[13]. Other factors, including the severity of the offense, the time that has elapsed since the offense has taken place, and the nature of the job must all be taken into account by the employer to determine if the applicant can be dismissed because of an arrest record. Keep in mind that rules regarding time limits on what a CRA can report vary from state to state, despite Federal regulation. As an example, under Federal law a CRA can report a conviction to an employer with no restriction on when the conviction occurred. However, there are eleven states which limit the reporting of a conviction to seven years. With that in mind, if you require additional information surrounding this topic then you should contact your state employment agency or office of consumer affairs.

The way this whole process works is that once a request is made by the employer to the CRA, the agency will then reach out to the candidate. The consumer reporting agency will ask the job candidate to fill out a questionnaire with basic information (name, DOB, SS#, names of past three employers, schools attended, etc). The CRA will then ask for your permission (and signature) to conduct the background check. The reason this is done is because certain information can only be procured with your permission. It can be an awkward feeling giving someone who you don't know, your most personal information. On top of that, knowing that a group of random people will be rummaging around in your past can be a bit discomforting. Unfortunately, it is what it is. If you don't give the CRA permission to conduct its job, you will almost certainly lose your job offer.

---

[13] U.S. Equal Employment Opportunity Commission. "Title VII of the Civil Rights Act of 1964" <https://www.eeoc.gov/laws/statutes/titlevii.cfm>

So bite your tongue, sign the documentation, and let the CRA carry out its job. Just know that you are not unique in this situation; background checks are common place these days with nearly 80%[14] of employers in the US conducting pre-employment screens.

On average, and in my experience, background checks take about 5-7 *business days* to complete from start to finish. For me this was always a gut wrenching week, while others may think nothing of it. By this point you will just want the whole interview process to be over and done with. You'll also be anxious to tell your current employer that you're headed for greener pastures. To that end, I strongly recommend not giving your notice, even if you have an offer in hand, until you have successfully passed the background check.

I have a few suggestions that may expedite the background check process. The first, and most obvious, is to return the questionnaire to the CRA as quickly as possible. Additionally, be mindful of the answers you provide in the questionnaire because the answers you provide could expedite or delay the CRA in its job. For instance, the questionnaire will undoubtedly require you to provide the phone numbers of your past three employers. Rather than simply writing down the "main" phone numbers to your previous employers (which could be a 1-800 number), be proactive and figure out exactly who at those companies the CRA will need to speak with. During my last background check I reached out to Human Resources at my last three employers. I simply asked who at the company is in charge of handling background check requests. I got that individual's direct contact information and put that name and number down on the background check questionnaire. This will help the CRA cut through the red tape, and ultimately save time.

Another tactic I recommend is to check in with the CRA a few days after returning your questionnaire. Typically the CRA will have provided you a point of contact which you can call with any questions you may have. I recommend giving the CRA a call four business days after submitting your paperwork to see if it is experiencing any issues procuring the information it needs to complete its work. It's unlikely the CRA will have completed its work at this time however, it's good to know where the CRA is hitting road blocks, if any. If for some reason the CRA indicates that it has been able to connect with all your prior employers except Company X (or school X), I suggest picking up the phone, calling your previous employer, or school,

---

[14] Sterling Talent Solutions. <http://www.sterlingtalentsolutions.com/About/About-Us>

and inquiring why the company has not been responsive to the inquires of the CRA. Don't worry about being a nuisance; you're not interviewing with your old employer. In my experiences I found it incredibly frustrating how long it took some of my ex-employers to provide the information needed to complete the background check, but such is life.

Once the background check is completed, and delivered to the employer, the employer should alert you (likely within 1-2 days) that the background check was completed to satisfaction. So all in, you could be looking at 7-10 business days to complete the whole process. For me, this period always felt like an eternity. Although I had nothing to hide in my past, I was aware that false information can accidentally surface in a background check. In recent years lawsuits have been filed against CRAs by job seekers that had offers rescinded due to inaccurate information that was provided to employers. The reason such errors arise is that CRAs are relying on information systems, rather than manual labor, to search record databases. Although technology can be efficient, it can also lead to errors. Don't get worked up about this, although these errors can occur, they are rare.

I am dedicating a substantial portion of time discussing background checks not to get you nervous, but rather to make you aware that a background check will occur, and how the process works. You should always assume that a background check will be completed following an offer, and with that in mind, you should assume that false information on your resume will likely surface. So, very simply put, don't lie on your resume. I am well aware that job candidates tend to use colorful adjectives on their resumes to spruce up the importance of their roles, and hiring managers are aware of this too. However, I'm not talking about using over the top adjectives here, I'm talking about misstating facts with the intent to deceive. Saying you went to school X, when you really attended school Y is deceptive. Saying you received a bachelor's degree in X, when you really only received an Associate's degree in X, is deceptive. Saying you achieved designation X, when you're still in the process of trying to secure designation X, is also deceptive. I think you catch my drift here. You should assume lies like these, and lies of a similar nature, will come to surface, and likely lead to a withdrawal of your job offer, so avoid making this easy mistake.

The next logical question you're probably asking yourself is whether or not it is okay to "stretch the truth" on one's resume? Stretching the truth is like walking a tight rope, so be very careful in your choice of words. Any statement which can be construed as misleading or untruthful is completely unacceptable. To clarify, I will provide an example of a job seeker stretching the truth on his resume, and then we'll discuss how such statements may be perceived.

Mike is an employee at the Oil Change Depot. Assume Mike's store is one of thousands of Oil Change Depots across the country, and all are wholly owned by a publicly traded energy company called Super Duper Oil Company. Mike's store performs high volume auto maintenance (e.g., oil changes, transmission fluid changes, etc). Mike's primary responsibilities in his job are to wash the oil rags, clean the store, and check all equipment at the end of the day. His title is "Maintenance Technician". He is very good at his job. Mike is exploring new opportunities and has constructed a resume. In describing his role as a Maintenance Technician, Mike writes the following in his resume:

- o *Through the reduction in utility rag wash cycle times and the use of lower cost cleaning products, improved store operating margins by 1%, directly leading to an appreciation of Super Duper Oil Company's common stock over the last 12 months.*

Is Mike making a false statement? Maybe he is, but then again, maybe he's not. Did Mike really move the needle on his parent company's share price? I don't think that question can be answered with a high degree of certainty, and Mike is likely making some major assumptions. So at the end of the day if I'm a hiring manager I would assume Mike did have an impact, albeit a modest one, on his stores's bottom line which in turn had some de minims impact on his parent company's stock price.

Although unlikely to be checked by a CRA, the validity of Mike's statement may be called into question during a reference check or in the interview. In summary, if you state what is perceived to be a fact on your resume, you must be able to back it up with evidence. In our example, Mike must be able to explain to the interviewer how he reached his conclusions. A rule of thumb is that you should always assume that someone will question every single detail on your resume, whether it be a date, a title, grade point average, an extracurricular activity, a job responsibility, or your middle initial, I mean every last detail. Follow that rule, and you'll be in good shape.

Chapter 15: Resigning

Congratulations, you're almost at the finish line, put the champagne on ice. Your background check has come back great, you have received a written offer from the company, and you know your start date. The last task you must perform is to tell your boss that you're moving on to the next chapter of your career. I've had this talk four times in my career, and I've never enjoyed it, but in certain instances it was more difficult than others. Call me over prepared, but I have always put some serious thought about how to approach my managers on this topic. Others are more impulsive, and may choose to just run into their manager's office and say whatever comes to mind. Before you go the latter route, take a deep breath. For just a moment, place yourself in your manager's shoes. By you leaving your post, you're causing hardship for your manager, and the company for that matter. Once you leave your manager will likely need to find your replacement, along with the arduous tasks of recruiting, interviewing, hiring, and training a new employee. By you leaving it inadvertently puts a lot of extra work on your manager's plate. Furthermore, your manager may have invested a great deal of time in training you, and perhaps had visions of you growing within the organization into bigger and better roles. Therefore, your manager may be feeling a mix of emotions due to your departure. Keep that in mind when giving your notice. I recommend covering the following bases during your resignation:

1. Thank your manager for giving you the opportunity to work at the firm.
2. Tell your manager that you valued the experience and what you've taken away from the position.
3. If asked, disclose your new company and role, but keep it brief. Don't try to justify the new position you have taken.
4. If asked why you're leaving the company or job, be courteous and respectful in your response. No matter how much you dislike your manager, it is not in your best interest to say something rude on your way out the door. Never burn bridges in business because you never know under what circumstance you may need to deal with your former manager/employer again.

I'm sure there are plenty of you out there that are reading this that truly dislike your job, and possibly your boss too. If you happen to fall into this category then skip topic #2 on the list above, as there is no need to be disingenuous during your exit interview. However, regardless of your situation, you need to be professional, which means giving your notice in such a way which is not going to offend anyone.

The Counteroffer

Finally, there is always the chance that your manager will try to get you to stay with the firm. Maybe he tries to lure you with more money or a new position. I've been offered, but never accepted a counter offer from a company I was leaving. My reasoning in not accepting a counter offer was simple. When deciding to leave a company I knew I was progressing forward in my career, sometimes even at a monetary sacrifice. Staying in a job simply because I would be receiving a salary bump was never enticing to me, personally. I always kept my long term goals in mind, and short term monetary incentives were never enough to deter me from those goals. However I do have friends who have accepted the "counter offer" just as they were about to head for the door, and are comfortable with their decision in doing so. Yet, if you were to ask them (which I have), they would admittedly state that they could have made more money in the long run had they decided to leave the company, take a new job, and gain more experience. Sometimes the allure of an immediate pay raise along with the comfort one finds in an existing job is enough to make someone stick around, rather than venturing into the unknown and having to reestablish one's self at a new firm. Every counteroffer and everyone's personal situation is different, so I can't say with certainty what decision you should make. The key take aways from this section are knowing that a counteroffer may be coming your way, and never ever accept a counter offer without giving yourself adequate time to think it through.

Epilogue

We've covered a lot of material in this book and I hope you've found it to be useful. I have provided you with the very same techniques that I used during three successful job searches between 2009 and 2013 (two of which were smack in the middle of the Great Financial Recession). There is nothing revolutionary about any one of the job searching techniques we have covered, yet when you put them all together you have a fully vetted blueprint for securing your next job. As I stated in the introduction of this book, I am not a career coach, recruiter, nor do I work in human resources. I am simply a job seeker, just like you, that has developed an effective method of securing employment. I did not develop this method easily, or without fault. I stumbled many a times in my quest for a new job, and made more mistakes over the years than I would care to count. I'm hoping my job searching techniques will allow you to circumvent those same mistakes that so many of us make along the path to employment.

Before we part ways I want to leave you with the following: Job searching is not easy, plain and simple. Job searching is a job in itself, and that is how you should approach this undertaking. Like any other job, to be truly successful your search will require hard work, sacrifice, dedication, and more. Earlier in this book I quoted a speaker from my graduation commencement, and given how true that statement is, it bears saying again - "Sometimes in life, to get ahead, you need to place yourself in uncomfortable situations." Holding true to those words, you too are likely to find yourself in situations throughout your job search that pull you out of your comfort zone. Yet remember, when you find yourself in those uncomfortable situations keep your eye on the prize, because landing that dream job will be nothing short of a fulfilling experience.

And finally, I know I'm supposed to say, "good luck" and let you begin your journey, but I'm not going to do that. Luck, in my opinion, is not some magical anomaly that few tend to experience, but rather a by-product of your hard work and perseverance.

I would like to say a special thank you to Ms. Susan Drevitch Kelly for her contributions to this book.

<u>Notes</u>